USEFUL PATCHWORK

CONTENTS

NO.1

Prologue

You'll find a rich variety of patchworks in this book. Why don't you choose your favorites and make them? They'll bring a touch of beauty to your daily life.

Flower Apron and Spool Bag

Instructions on page 2.

NO.2

Materials No. 1: White, 1m(39⅜″) by 70cm(27⅝″); fabric for patterns, a little; fabric for lining and cotton fabric, 60cm(23⅝″) by 35cm(13¾″) each. No. 2: Black, Inner bag fabric, fabric for lining and cotton fabric, 60cm(23⅝″) by 40cm(15¾″) each; fabric for patterns, a little; 25cm(10″) zipper, handle string, 50cm(19⅝″) .

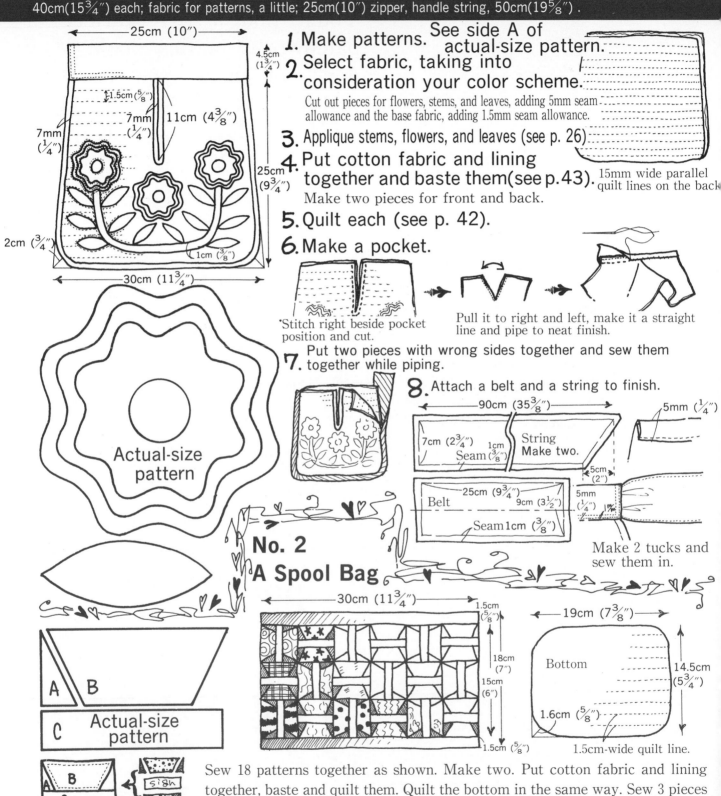

1. Make patterns. See side A of actual-size pattern.
2. Select fabric, taking into consideration your color scheme.
   Cut out pieces for flowers, stems, and leaves, adding 5mm seam allowance and the base fabric, adding 1.5mm seam allowance.
3. Applique stems, flowers, and leaves (see p. 26)
4. Put cotton fabric and lining together and baste them(see p.43). Make two pieces for front and back.
5. Quilt each (see p. 42).
6. Make a pocket.

Stitch right beside pocket position and cut.   Pull it to right and left, make it a straight line and pipe to neat finish.

7. Put two pieces with wrong sides together and sew them together while piping.

8. Attach a belt and a string to finish.

15mm wide parallel quilt lines on the back

25cm (10″)
4.5cm (1¾″)
1.5cm (⅝″)
7mm (¼″) 11cm (4⅜″)
7mm (¼″)
25cm (9¾″)
2cm (¾″)
1cm (⅜″)
30cm (11¾″)

Actual-size pattern

90cm (35⅜″)
5mm (¼″)
7cm (2¾″) 1cm Seam (⅜″) String Make two.
5cm (2″)
25cm (9¾″) 5mm (¼″)
Belt 9cm (3½″)
Seam1cm (⅜″)
Make 2 tucks and sew them in.

No. 2
A Spool Bag

A B
C Actual-size pattern

30cm (11¾″)
1.5cm (⅝″)
18cm (7″)
15cm (6″)
1.5cm (⅝″)

19cm (7⅜″)
Bottom
14.5cm (5¾″)
1.6cm (⅝″)
1.5cm-wide quilt line.

B
A
C
3mm (⅛″)
sish

Sew 18 patterns together as shown. Make two. Put cotton fabric and lining together, baste and quilt them. Quilt the bottom in the same way. Sew 3 pieces together to make a bag. Put and sew zipper to opening and sew a handle (a cord sold on the market is OK) on the sides. Make inner bag in the same size and sew it beside the zipper.

Materials   Nos. 114–116: fabric for patterns, a little; cotton fabric and fabric for lining, 80cm(31⅜″) by 50cm(19⅝″) each; synthetic cotton, proper quantity; brick, 1; beads for eyes, 2   Nos. 117–118: fabric for patterns, a little; cotton fabric and fabric for lining, 1m(39⅜″) by 70cm(27⅝″) each.

1. Make patterns.

2. Select fabric, taking into consideration your color scheme.

Cut out triangles, adding 7mm-seam allowance and others adding 1cm-seam allowance.

3. Piece work a triangle.

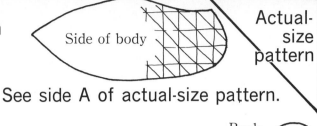

See side A of actual-size pattern.

The other must be in reverse. Be careful.

4. Put cotton fabric and fabric for lining to twt body sides and one bottom respectively and baste carefully (see p. 43).

Draw 2cm-wide check quilt line on the front side of fabric with sharpend 2B pencil.

5. Quilt (see p. 42).

6. Make two pieces of a beak, a head and the body side sewed together. Put them and bottom with right side together and sew them except opening for turning.

7. Put synthetic cotton and weight inside, sew the opening and close it.

Wrap something heavy with cotton and put it inside. For example, a stone or a brick, clay, etc.

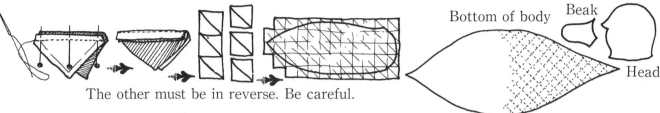

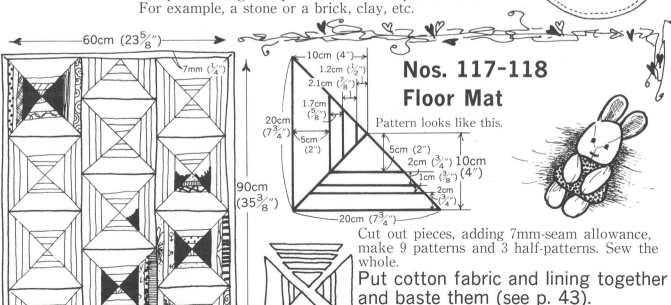

60cm (23⅝″)

7mm (¼″)

90cm (35⅜″)

Nos. 117–118
Floor Mat

Pattern looks like this.

10cm (4″)
1.2cm (½″)
2.1cm (⅞″)
1.7cm (⅝″)
20cm (7¾″)
5cm (2″)
5cm (2″)
2cm (¾″) 10cm (4″)
1cm (⅜″)
2cm (¾″)
20cm (7¾″)

Cut out pieces, adding 7mm-seam allowance, make 9 patterns and 3 half-patterns. Sew the whole.

Put cotton fabric and lining together and baste them (see p. 43).

Quilt (see p. 42).

Pipe around the ebge and it's done (see p. 50).

3

Arrow Tree Tapestry

This is a gorgeous addition to a living room wall.
This color scheme can be used year=round.
It matches the oak-wood work.

**instructions
on page 6.**

Chair Cushion

These two cushions have reveres color patterns. The different patterns are eye-catching, aren't they? With patchwork you can enjoy making such an interesting contrast.

NO.4

Instructions on page 7.

Arrow Tree Tapestry P. 4

Materials

No. 3; fabric for patterns, a little; cotton fabric and fabric for lining—1m(39⅜″) by 1m(39⅜″) each.

94cm (37″)

16cm (6⅜″)

56cm (22″)

16cm (6⅜″)

25cm (9¾″)

3cm (1⅛″)

25cm (9¾″)

3cm (1⅛″)

31cm (12¼″)

2cm (¾″)

1.5cm-wide quilt line.

94 cm (37″)

See side A of actual-size pattern.

After sewing each block, sew the whole together.

1. Make patterns.

2. Select fabric, taking into consideration your color scheme.

Because there are many pieces, it is very hard to select fabric.

It may be easier if you select a color from the center.

After selecting fabric cut out pieces, adding 7mm seam allowance

3. Piece work.

Applique arrows, leaves, circles and squares (see p. 26).

Draw stems in outline stitch (see p.54)

Sew to mark at ( )

4. Put cotton fabric and lining together and baste them (see p. 43).

5. Quilt (see p. 42).

6. Pipe around the edge (see p. 50).

Fight!

Materials

No. 4: red and white, 1m(39⅜″) by 1m(39⅜″) each; cotton fabric and fabric for lining, 1m(39⅜″) by 50cm(19⅝″) each; 35cm(13¾″) zipper

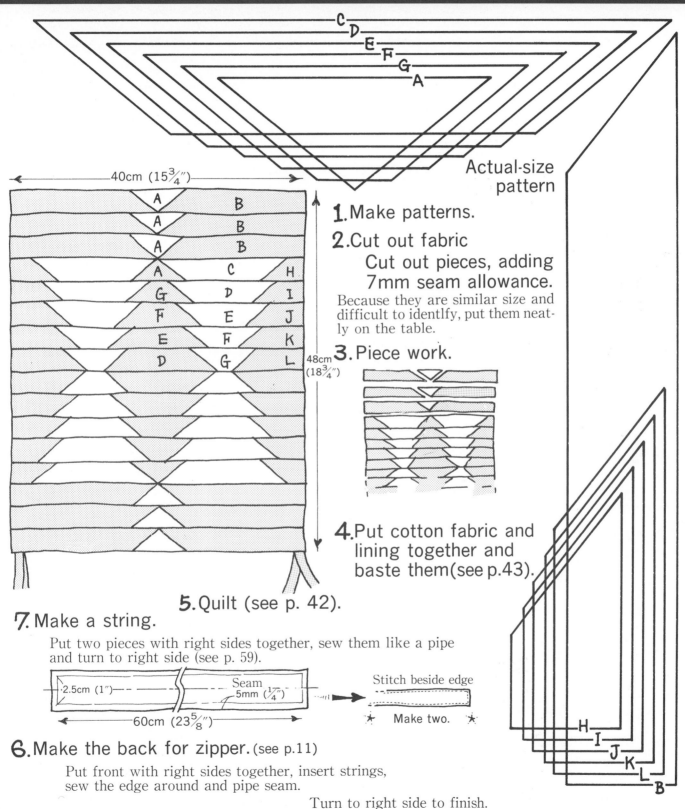

Actual-size pattern

40cm (15¾″)

48cm (18¾″)

1. Make patterns.

2. Cut out fabric

Cut out pieces, adding 7mm seam allowance.

Because they are similar size and difficult to identlfy, put them neatly on the table.

3. Piece work.

4. Put cotton fabric and lining together and baste them(see p.43).

5. Quilt (see p. 42).

7. Make a string.

Put two pieces with right sides together, sew them like a pipe and turn to right side (see p. 59).

2.5cm (1″)

Seam 5mm (¼″)

60cm (23⅝″)

Stitch beside edge

★ Make two. ★

6. Make the back for zipper.(see p.11)

Put front with right sides together, insert strings, sew the edge around and pipe seam.

Turn to right side to finish.

NO.5

NO.8

NO.9

8

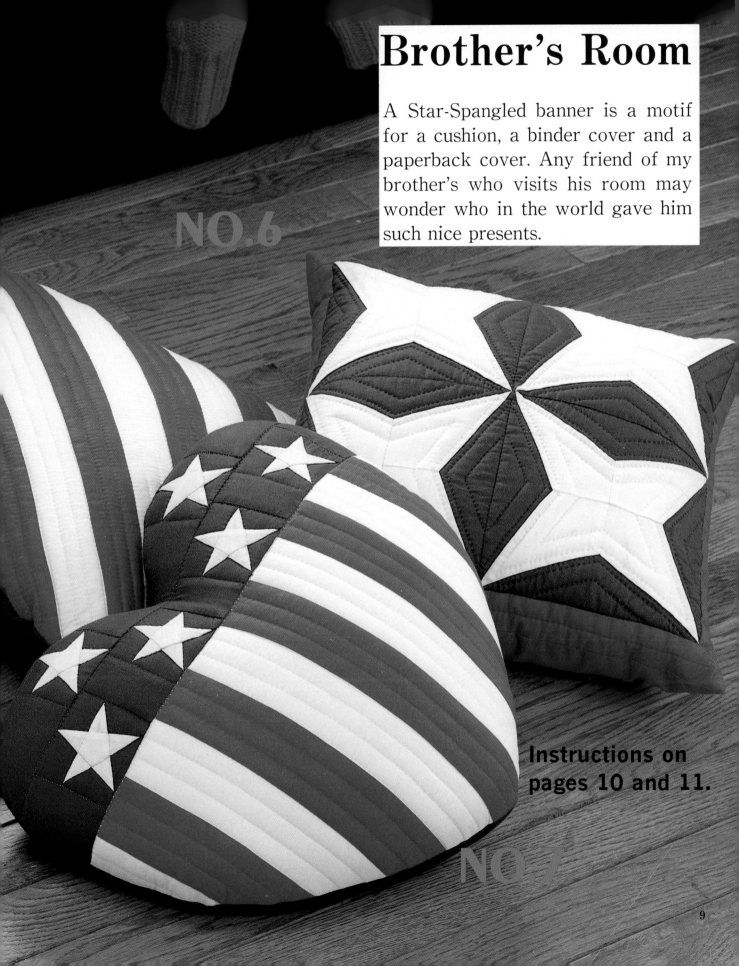

Brother's Room

A Star-Spangled banner is a motif for a cushion, a binder cover and a paperback cover. Any friend of my brother's who visits his room may wonder who in the world gave him such nice presents.

Instructions on pages 10 and 11.

Materials: No. 5: red and white. 70cm(27⅝″) by 40cm(15¾″) each; dark blue. 1m(39⅜″) by 70cm(27⅝″); 30cm(11¾″) zipper; inner bag, 1m(39⅜″) by 50cm(19⅝″); synthetic cotton, proper quantity   No. 6: dark blue, white, cotton fabric and fabric for lining, 50cm(19⅝″) by 50cm(19⅝″) each; red, 70cm(27⅝″) by 70cm(27⅝″) each; inner bag, 1m by 50cm(19⅝″); 30cm(11¾″) zipper; synthetic cotton, proper quantity   No. 7; dark blue,

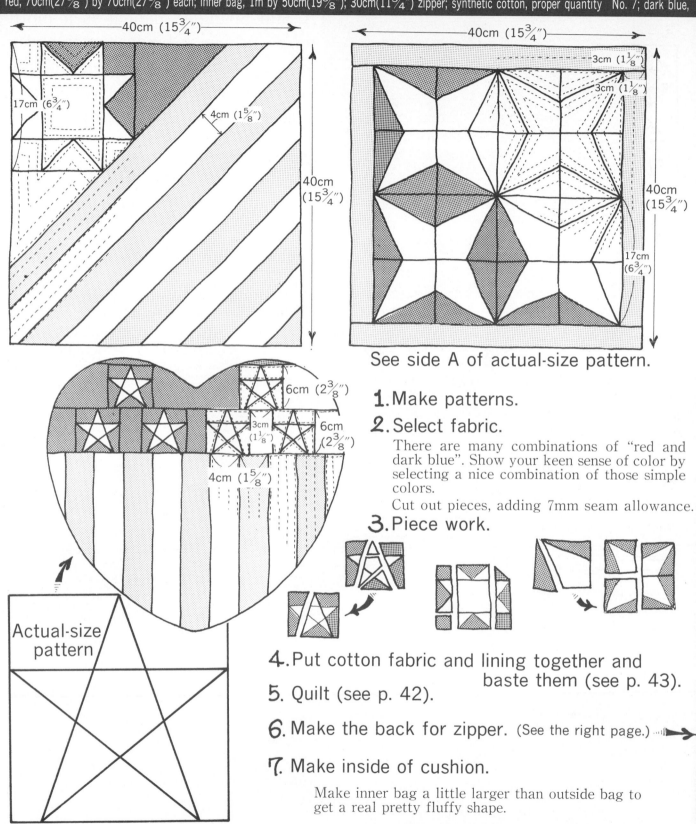

See side A of actual-size pattern.

1. Make patterns.

2. Select fabric.

There are many combinations of "red and dark blue". Show your keen sense of color by selecting a nice combination of those simple colors.

Cut out pieces, adding 7mm seam allowance.

3. Piece work.

4. Put cotton fabric and lining together and baste them (see p. 43).

5. Quilt (see p. 42).

6. Make the back for zipper. (See the right page.)

7. Make inside of cushion.

Make inner bag a little larger than outside bag to get a real pretty fluffy shape.

Actual-size pattern

70cm(27⅝″) by 70cm(27⅝″); white, red, cotton fabric and fabric for lining, 50cm(19⅝″) by 50cm(19⅝″) each; inner bag, 1m(39⅜″) by 50cm(19⅝″); 30cm(11¾″) zipper; synthetic cotton, proper quantity No. 8: white, 1m50cm(59″) by 50cm(19⅝″); red, 50cm(19⅝″) by 50cm(19⅝″); cotton fabric, 50cm(19⅝″) by 40cm(15¾″); No. 9: white, 70cm(27⅝″) by 30cm(11¾″); blue, 30cm(11¾″) by 30cm(11¾″); cotton fabric, 30cm(11¾″) by 20cm(7¾″)

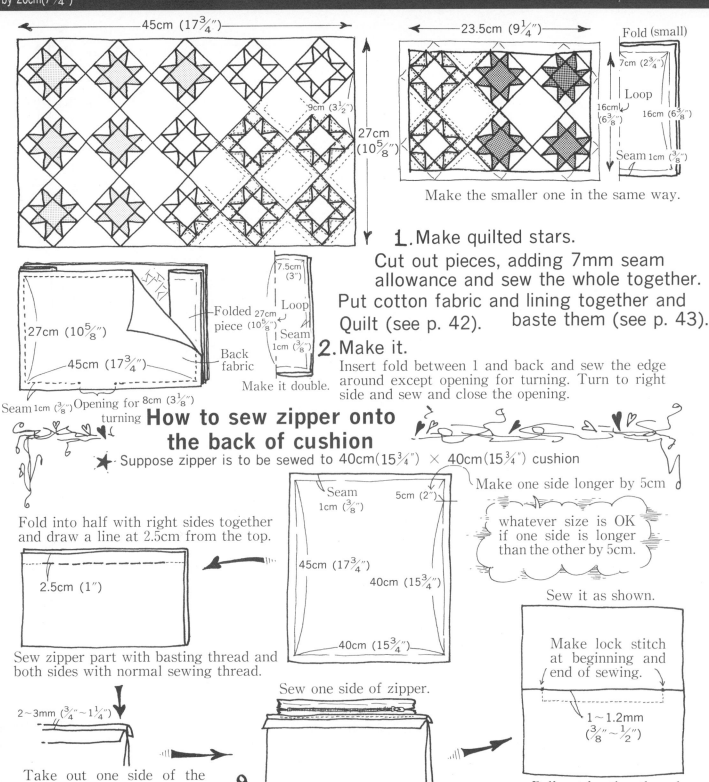

45cm (17¾″)

23.5cm (9¼″)

Fold (small)

7cm (2¾″)

Loop

16cm (6⅜″)   16cm (6⅜″)

Seam 1cm (⅜″)

27cm (10⅝″)

9cm (3½″)

Make the smaller one in the same way.

1. Make quilted stars.

Cut out pieces, adding 7mm seam allowance and sew the whole together. Put cotton fabric and lining together and Quilt (see p. 42).   baste them (see p. 43).

2. Make it.

Insert fold between 1 and back and sew the edge around except opening for turning. Turn to right side and sew and close the opening.

7.5cm (3″)

Folded 27cm (10⅝″) piece   Loop

Back fabric   Seam 1cm (⅜″)

27cm (10⅝″)

45cm (17¾″)

Seam 1cm (⅜″) Opening for 8cm (3⅛″) turning

Make it double.

How to sew zipper onto the back of cushion

★ Suppose zipper is to be sewed to 40cm(15¾″) × 40cm(15¾″) cushion

Fold into half with right sides together and draw a line at 2.5cm from the top.

2.5cm (1″)

Sew zipper part with basting thread and both sides with normal sewing thread.

Seam 1cm (⅜″)

5cm (2″)

45cm (17¾″)

40cm (15¾″)

40cm (15¾″)

Make one side longer by 5cm

whatever size is OK if one side is longer than the other by 5cm.

Sew it as shown.

Make lock stitch at beginning and end of sewing.

1~1.2mm (⅜″~½″)

2~3mm (¾″~1¼″)

Take out one side of the seam by 2-3mm and fold it as shown.

Sew one side of zipper.

Cut a folded side and open it.

Pull out basting thread to finish.

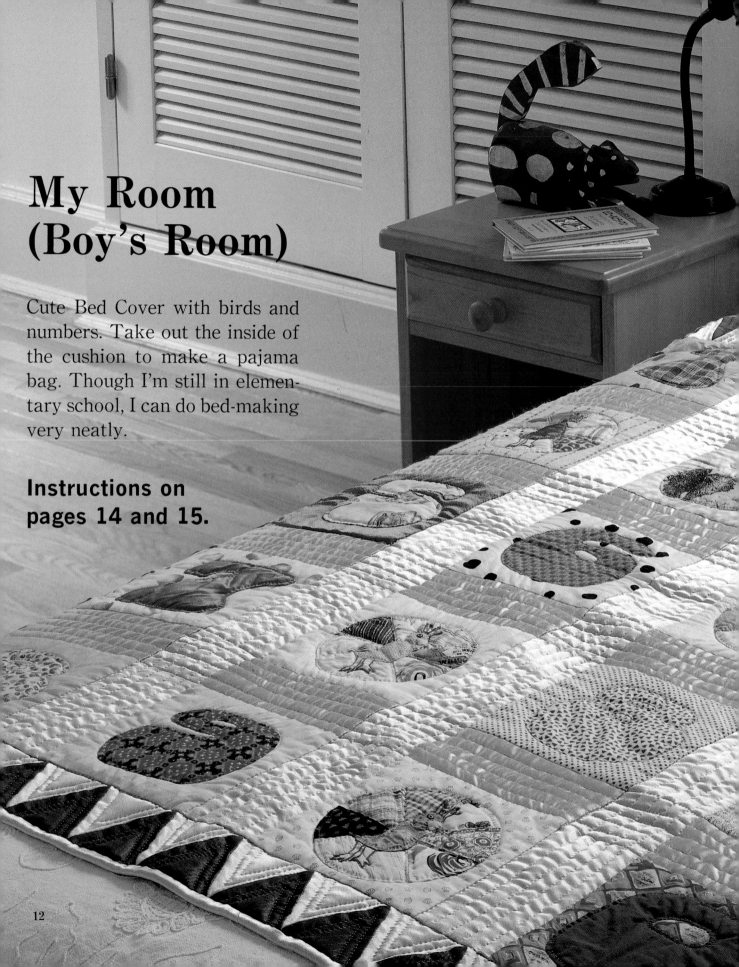

My Room
(Boy's Room)

Cute Bed Cover with birds and numbers. Take out the inside of the cushion to make a pajama bag. Though I'm still in elementary school, I can do bed-making very neatly.

**Instructions on
pages 14 and 15.**

12

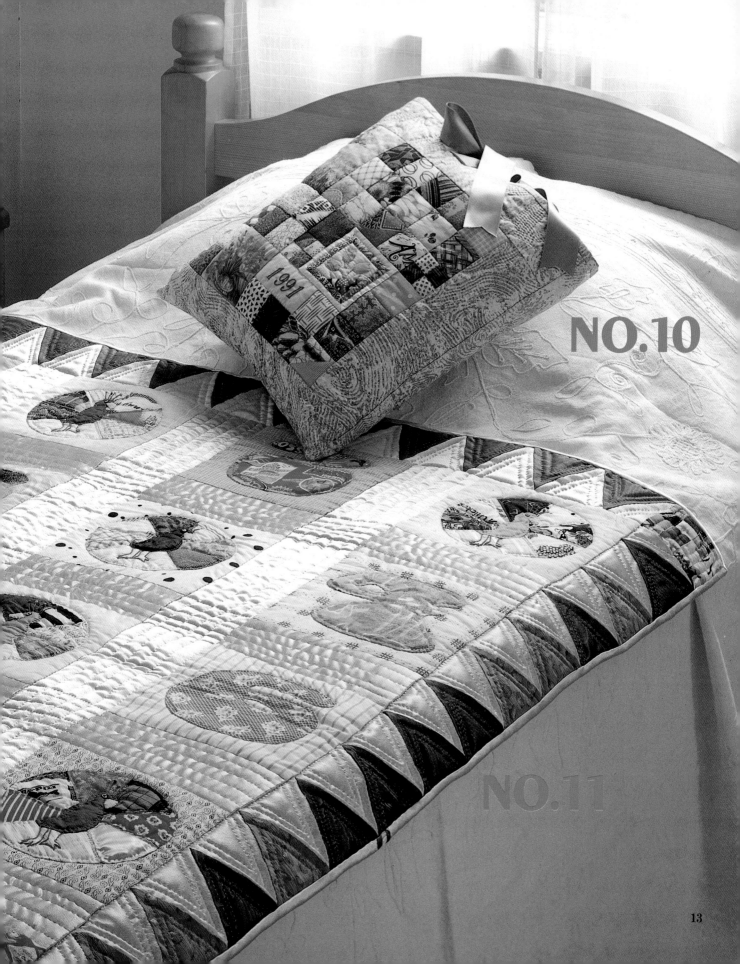

NO.10

NO.11

My Room (Boy's Room)　PP. 12, 13

Materials No. 10: fabric for patterns, a little; front, 1m(39⅜″) by 50cm(19⅝″); cotton fabric and fabric for lining, 50cm(19⅝″) by 50cm(19⅝″) each; synthetic cotton, proper quantity; 4cm(1⅝″)-wide ribbon, 120cm(47¼″)

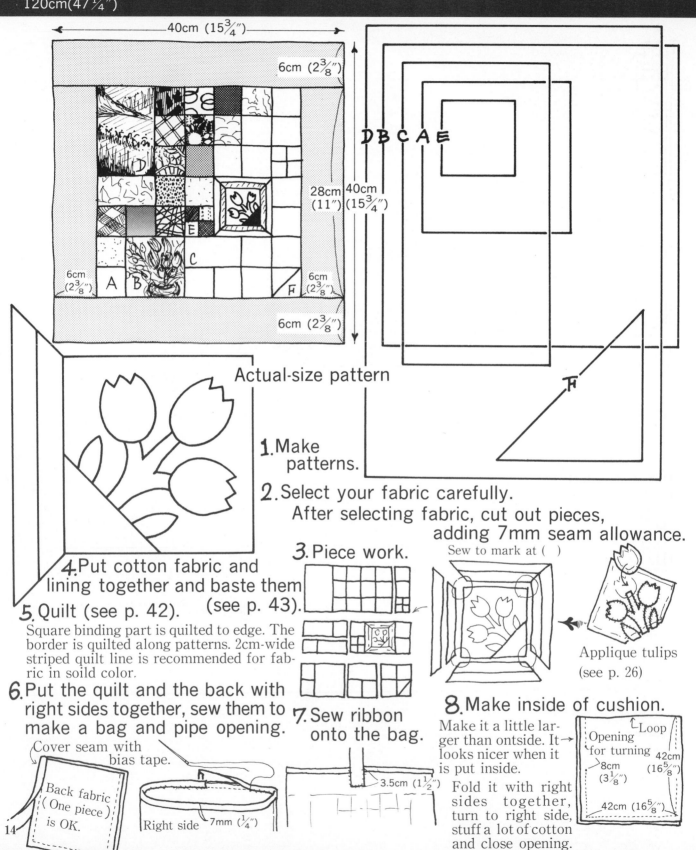

40cm (15¾″)

6cm (2⅜″)

28cm (11″)　40cm (15¾″)

6cm (2⅜″)

6cm (2⅜″)

6cm (2⅜″)

D B C A E

F

Actual-size pattern

1. Make patterns.

2. Select your fabric carefully. After selecting fabric, cut out pieces, adding 7mm seam allowance.

3. Piece work.

Sew to mark at ( )

Applique tulips (see p. 26)

4. Put cotton fabric and lining together and baste them (see p. 43).

5. Quilt (see p. 42).

Square binding part is quilted to edge. The border is quilted along patterns. 2cm-wide striped quilt line is recommended for fabric in soild color.

6. Put the quilt and the back with right sides together, sew them to make a bag and pipe opening.

Cover seam with bias tape.

Back fabric (One piece) is OK.

Right side 7mm (¼″)

7. Sew ribbon onto the bag.

3.5cm (1½″)

8. Make inside of cushion.

Make it a little larger than ontside. It looks nicer when it is put inside.

Fold it with right sides together, turn to right side, stuff a lot of cotton and close opening.

Loop

Opening for turning　42cm (16⅝″)

8cm (3⅛″)

42cm (16⅝″)

14

No. 11: fabric for patterns, a little; cotton fabric and fabric for lining, 1m50cm(59″) by 1m30cm(51⅜″) each

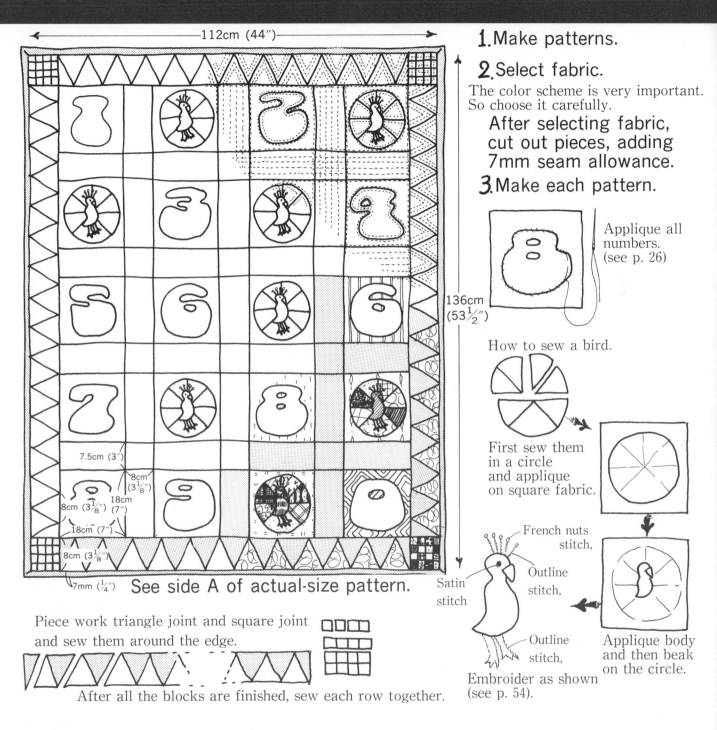

←————— 112cm (44″) —————→

136cm (53½″)

7.5cm (3″)

8cm (3⅛″)

8cm (3⅛″) 18cm (7″)

18cm (7″)

8cm (3⅛″)

7mm (¼″)

See side A of actual-size pattern.

1. Make patterns.

2. Select fabric.

The color scheme is very important. So choose it carefully.

After selecting fabric, cut out pieces, adding 7mm seam allowance.

3. Make each pattern.

Applique all numbers. (see p. 26)

How to sew a bird.

First sew them in a circle and applique on square fabric.

Applique body and then beak on the circle.

French nuts stitch,

Outline stitch,

Satin stitch

Outline stitch,

Embroider as shown (see p. 54).

Piece work triangle joint and square joint and sew them around the edge.

After all the blocks are finished, sew each row together.

Draw quilt line with sharpened 2B pencil.

Keep a pencil sharpener at hand.

4. Put cotton fabric and lining together and baste them (see p. 43).

5. Quilt carefully (see. p. 42).

6. Pipe around the ebge and it's done (see p. 50).

15

Instructions on
pages 18 and 19.

16

Welcome to Our Home

Cat and owl mother and child are mascots that extend a hearty welcome to any visitors. They look so good=humored that everybody loves to hold them.

NO.13

NO.14

Welcome to Our Home pp.16, 17

Materials No. 12: fabric for patterns, a little; white, 60cm(23⅜″) by 50cm(19⅝″), cotton fabric and fabric for lining, 1m(39⅜″) by 50cm(19⅝″); No. 25 embroidery thread, a little, 1.2cm(½″)-wide ribbon, 1m(39⅜″); one bell; synthetic cotton, proper quantity

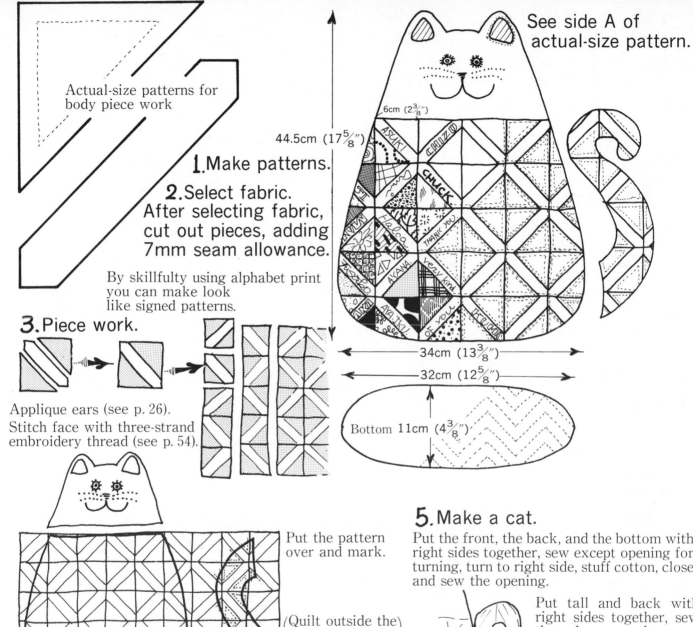

Actual-size patterns for body piece work

44.5cm (17⅝″)

See side A of actual-size pattern.

6cm (2⅜″)

1. Make patterns.

2. Select fabric.
After selecting fabric, cut out pieces, adding 7mm seam allowance.

By skillfulty using alphabet print you can make look like signed patterns.

3. Piece work.

Applique ears (see p. 26).
Stitch face with three-strand embroidery thread (see p. 54).

34cm (13⅜″)

32cm (12⅝″)

Bottom 11cm (4⅜″)

Put the pattern over and mark.

(Quilt outside the mark by 7mm.)

4. Put cotton fabric and lining together, baste (see p. 43) and quilt (see p. 42).

The back and back of the tail are onepiece.
The same quilt line with the bottom on one piece.

5. Make a cat.
Put the front, the back, and the bottom with right sides together, sew except opening for turning, turn to right side, stuff cotton, close and sew the opening.

Put tall and back with right sides together, sew the edge around except opening for turning, turn to right side, stuff cotton and close opening.

Sew the tall to the tail position.

First sew the bottom and sew the top.

Put a ribbon and a bell to finish.

No. 13: brown, 50cm(19⅝″) by 50cm(19⅝″); fabric for patterns, a little; cotton fabric and fabric for lining, 70cm(27⅝″) by 40cm(15¾″); No. 25 embroidery thread, a little; synthetic cotton, proper quantity

No. 14: brown, 80cm(31⅜″) by 50cm(19⅝″); fabric for patterns, a little; cotton fabric and fabric for lining, 1m(39⅜″) by 50cm(19⅝″) each; No. 25 embroidery thread, a little; synthetic cotton, proper quantity

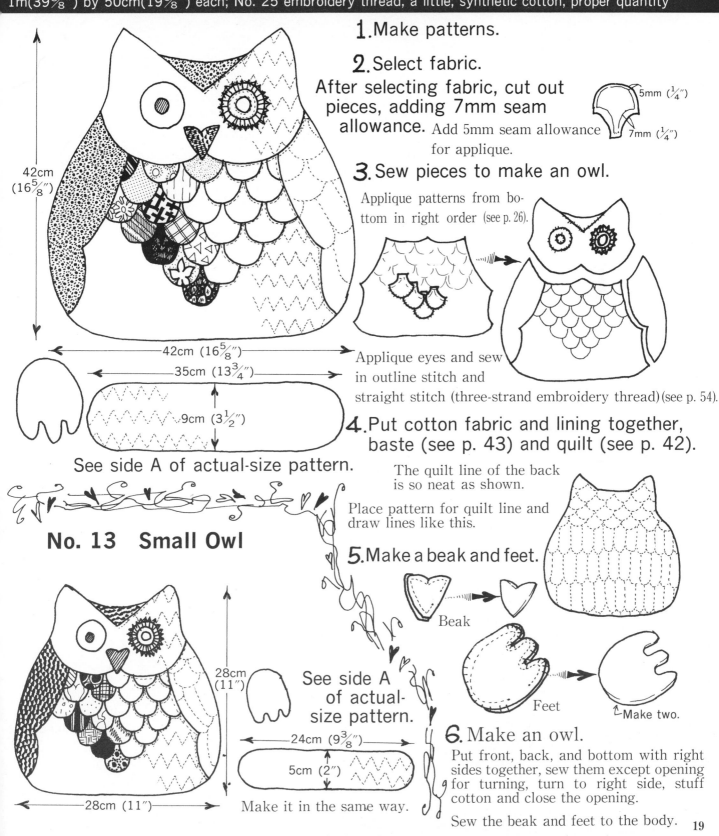

1. Make patterns.

2. Select fabric.

After selecting fabric, cut out pieces, adding 7mm seam allowance. Add 5mm seam allowance for applique.

5mm (¼″)

7mm (¼″)

3. Sew pieces to make an owl.

Applique patterns from bottom in right order (see p. 26).

Applique eyes and sew in outline stitch and straight stitch (three-strand embroidery thread) (see p. 54).

4. Put cotton fabric and lining together, baste (see p. 43) and quilt (see p. 42).

The quilt line of the back is so neat as shown.

Place pattern for quilt line and draw lines like this.

5. Make a beak and feet.

Beak

Feet

Make two.

6. Make an owl.

Put front, back, and bottom with right sides together, sew them except opening for turning, turn to right side, stuff cotton and close the opening.

Sew the beak and feet to the body.

42cm (16⅝″)

42cm (16⅝″)

35cm (13¾″)

9cm (3½″)

See side A of actual-size pattern.

No. 13   Small Owl

28cm (11″)

28cm (11″)

See side A of actual-size pattern.

24cm (9⅜″)

5cm (2″)

Make it in the same way.

19

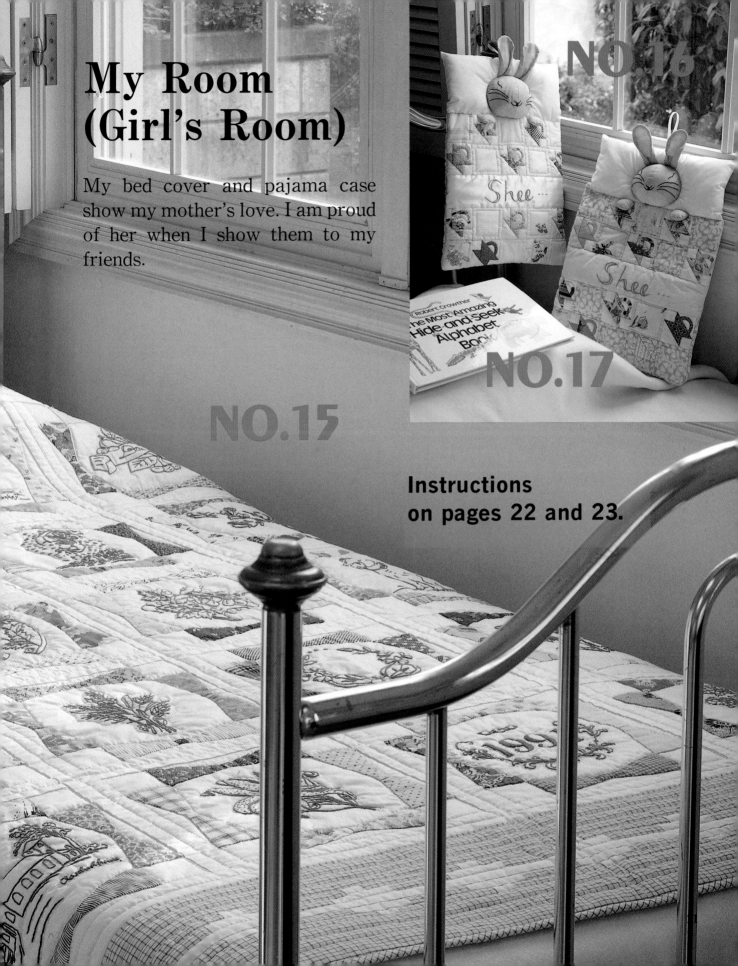

My Room
(Girl's Room)

My bed cover and pajama case
show my mother's love. I am proud
of her when I show them to my
friends.

NO. 16

Shee ...

NO.17

NO.15

**Instructions
on pages 22 and 23.**

My Room (Girl's Room) pp.20, 21

Materials

No. 15: white, blue check, cotton fabric and fabric for lining, 2m(78¾″) by 1m60cm(63″) each; fabric for patterns, a little; No. 25 embroidery thread, a little

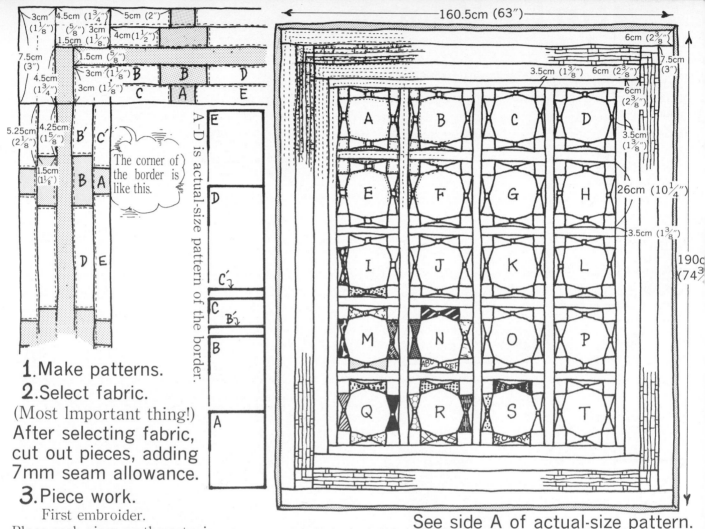

See side A of actual-size pattern.

1. Make patterns.
2. Select fabric.

(Most Important thing!)
After selecting fabric, cut out pieces, adding 7mm seam allowance.

3. Piece work.

First embroider.
Place each piece on the actual-size pattern and draw a picture on fabric with 2B pencil.

Embroider all in outline stitches (see p. 54).

Use three-strand embroidery thread.

Sew to mark at ( ).

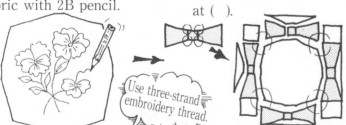

Sew to mark at ( ).

Join each row in the border.

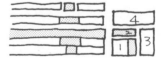

When each block has been sewn, sew and join the whole.

4. Put cotton fabric and lining together and baste them (see p. 43).

5. Quilt (see p. 42).

6. Pipe around the edge and it's done (see p. 50).

It takes a long time to finish each part, since it is so large, but you will have a real sense of accomplishment when you finish it.

Nos. 16, 17: white (including lining), 1m(39⅜″) by 70cm(27⅝″) each; fabric for patterns, a little; cotton fabric, 70cm(27⅝″) by 50cm(19⅝″); No. 25 embroidery thread, a little; 8cm(3⅛″)-wide ribbon, 20cm(7¾″); synthetic cotton, proper quantity

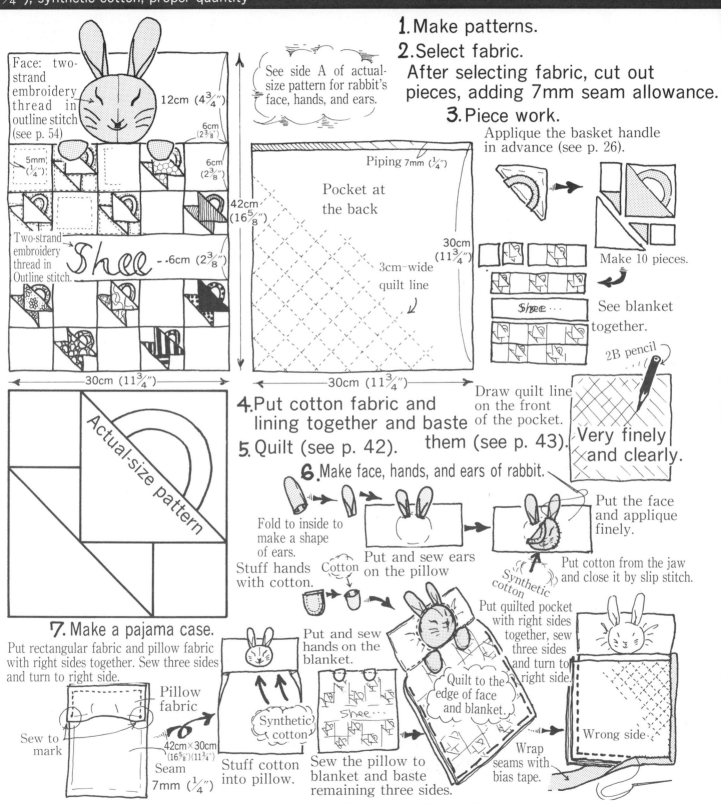

Face: two-strand embroidery thread in outline stitch (see p. 54)

5mm (¼″)

12cm (4¾″)

6cm (2⅜″)

6cm (2⅜″)

42cm (16⅝″)

Two-strand embroidery thread in Outline stitch.

Shee

6cm (2⅜″)

30cm (11¾″)

Actual-size pattern

See side A of actual-size pattern for rabbit's face, hands, and ears.

Piping 7mm (¼″)

Pocket at the back

3cm-wide quilt line

30cm (11¾″)

30cm (11¾″)

1. Make patterns.
2. Select fabric.
   After selecting fabric, cut out pieces, adding 7mm seam allowance.
3. Piece work.
   Applique the basket handle in advance (see p. 26).

Make 10 pieces.

Shee...

See blanket together.

2B pencil

Draw quilt line on the front of the pocket.

Very finely and clearly.

4. Put cotton fabric and lining together and baste them (see p. 43).
5. Quilt (see p. 42).
6. Make face, hands, and ears of rabbit.

Fold to inside to make a shape of ears.

Stuff hands with cotton.

Cotton

Put and sew ears on the pillow

Synthetic cotton

Put the face and applique finely.

Put cotton from the jaw and close it by slip stitch.

7. Make a pajama case.

Put rectangular fabric and pillow fabric with right sides together. Sew three sides and turn to right side.

Sew to mark

Pillow fabric

42cm×30cm (16⅝″)(11¾″)

Seam 7mm (¼″)

Stuff cotton into pillow.

Put and sew hands on the blanket.

Synthetic cotton

Shee...

Sew the pillow to blanket and baste remaining three sides.

Put quilted pocket with right sides together, sew three sides and turn to right side.

Quilt to the edge of face and blanket.

Wrap seams with bias tape.

Wrong side

Make hanging ribbon (6mm width by 20cm) in a loop and sew it to back.

23

Heart & Heart

A heart-shaped patchwork graces the wall of a warm-hearted home. The color scheme of the tapestry is fantastic. The soothing brown tones of the wall pocket and the tissue box cover create a peaceful atmospher. Be creative in finding the many different possible ways to use the wall pocket.

NO.19

NO.20

instructions on pages 26 and 27.

Materials

No. 18: fabric for patterns, a little; cotton fabric and fabric for lining, 1m(39⅜″) by 1m(39⅜″) each;

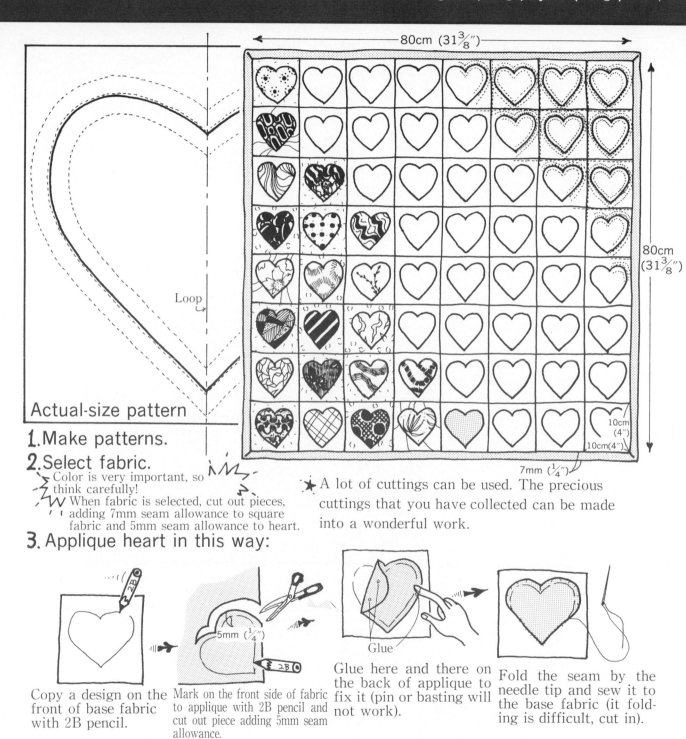

80cm (31⅜″)

80cm (31⅜″)

10cm (4″)

10cm(4″)

7mm (¼″)

Actual-size pattern

Loop

1. Make patterns.

2. Select fabric.

Color is very important, so think carefully!
When fabric is selected, cut out pieces, adding 7mm seam allowance to square fabric and 5mm seam allowance to heart.

★ A lot of cuttings can be used. The precious cuttings that you have collected can be made into a wonderful work.

3. Applique heart in this way:

5mm (¼″)

Glue

Copy a design on the front of base fabric with 2B pencil.

Mark on the front side of fabric to applique with 2B pencil and cut out piece adding 5mm seam allowance.

Glue here and there on the back of applique to fix it (pin or basting will not work).

Fold the seam by the needle tip and sew it to the base fabric (it folding is difficult, cut in).

When 64 hearts are made, sew the whole together.

4. Put cotton fabric and lining together and baste them (see p. 43).

5. Quilt carefully (see. p. 42).

6. Pipe around the ebge and it's done (see p. 50).

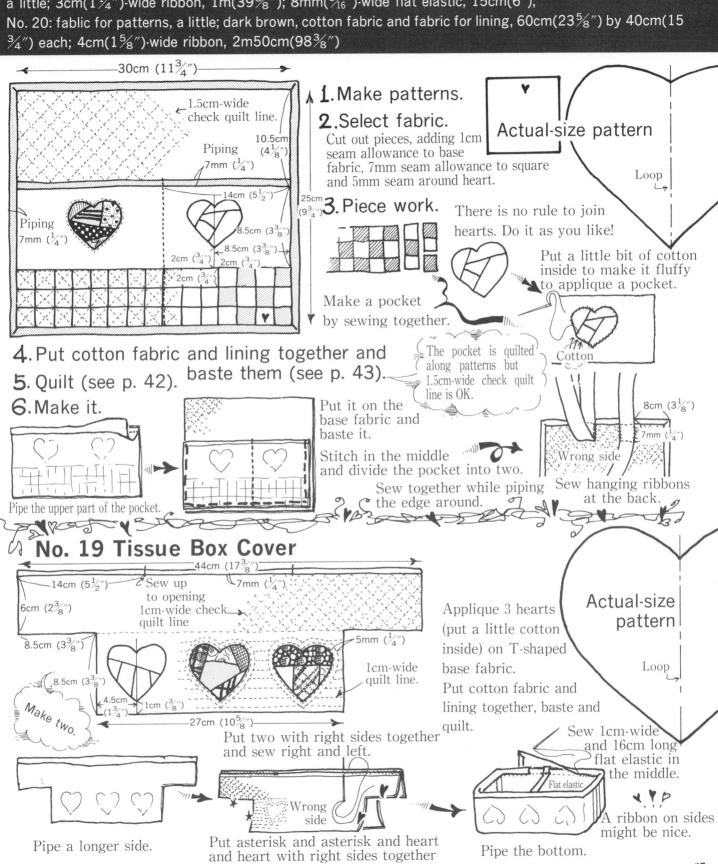

No. 19: front, cotton fabric and fabric for lining, 50cm(19⅝″) by 40cm(15¾″) each; fabric for patterns, a little; 3cm(1¼″)-wide ribbon, 1m(39⅜″); 8mm(5/16″)-wide flat elastic, 15cm(6″);
No. 20: fablic for patterns, a little; dark brown, cotton fabric and fabric for lining, 60cm(23⅝″) by 40cm(15¾″) each; 4cm(1⅝″)-wide ribbon, 2m50cm(98⅜″)

30cm (11¾″)

1.5cm-wide check quilt line.

10.5cm (4⅛″)

Piping 7mm (¼″)

14cm (5½″)

25cm (9¾″)

8.5cm (3⅜″)

Piping 7mm (¼″)

8.5cm (3⅜″)

2cm (¾″)   2cm (¾″)

2cm (¾″)

1. Make patterns.
2. Select fabric.
Cut out pieces, adding 1cm seam allowance to base fabric, 7mm seam allowance to square and 5mm seam around heart.

3. Piece work.

Actual-size pattern

Loop

There is no rule to join hearts. Do it as you like!

Put a little bit of cotton inside to make it fluffy to applique a pocket.

Make a pocket by sewing together.

Cotton

The pocket is quilted along patterns but 1.5cm-wide check quilt line is OK.

4. Put cotton fabric and lining together and baste them (see p. 43).
5. Quilt (see p. 42).
6. Make it.

Put it on the base fabric and baste it.

Stitch in the middle and divide the pocket into two.

Sew together while piping the edge around.

8cm (3⅛″)

7mm (¼″)

Wrong side

Sew hanging ribbons at the back.

Pipe the upper part of the pocket.

No. 19 Tissue Box Cover

44cm (17⅜″)

14cm (5½″)   Sew up to opening 1cm-wide check quilt line

7mm (¼″)

6cm (2⅜″)

8.5cm (3⅜″)

5mm (¼″)

8.5cm (3⅜″)

1cm-wide quilt line.

Make two.

4.5cm (1¾″)   1cm (⅜″)

27cm (10⅝″)

Applique 3 hearts (put a little cotton inside) on T-shaped base fabric.

Put cotton fabric and lining together, baste and quilt.

Actual-size pattern

Loop

Put two with right sides together and sew right and left.

Pipe a longer side.

Wrong side

Put asterisk and asterisk and heart and heart with right sides together and sew them.
Pipe seams.

Sew 1cm-wide and 16cm long flat elastic in the middle.

Flat elastic

Pipe the bottom.

A ribbon on sides might be nice.

27

NO.21

NO.22

Dahlia in Winter

Hot milk and homemade cake at tea-time...
The tablecloth and teapot cover are also homemade.
Luncheon mat has a pocket with dahlia pattern.

**Instruction on
pages 30 and 31.**

Dahlia in Winter pp. 28, 29

Materials

No. 21: white, 30cm(11¾″) by 30cm(11¾″); fabric for patterns, a little; cotton fabric and fabric for lining, 50cm(19⅝″) by 30cm(11¾″) each

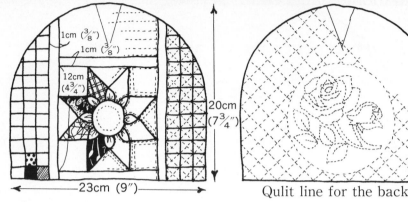

See side B of actual-size pattern.

1cm (⅜″)
1cm (⅜″)
12cm (4¾″)
20cm (7¾″)
23cm (9″)

Qulit line for the back

1. Make patterns.

2. Select fabric.

Cut out pieces, adding 7mm seam allowance each for the front.

Cut out pieces, adding 1cm seam allowance for the back and copy a design with 2B pencil.

If you chose fabric in a dark color, put a design and the fabric on the window glass and copy the design

3. Piece work.

Sew to mark at ( ).

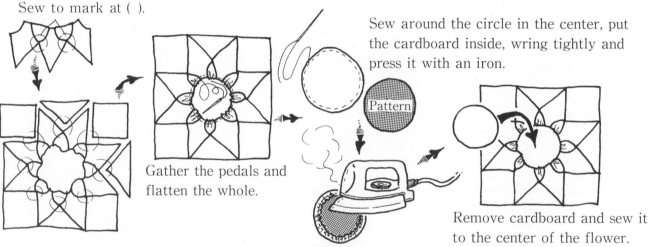

Gather the pedals and flatten the whole.

Sew around the circle in the center, put the cardboard inside, wring tightly and press it with an iron.

Pattern

Remove cardboard and sew it to the center of the flower.

4. Put cotton fabric and lining together, baste (see p. 43) and quilt (see p. 42) for front and back respectively.

(see p. 43) ... (see p. 42)

5. Make it.

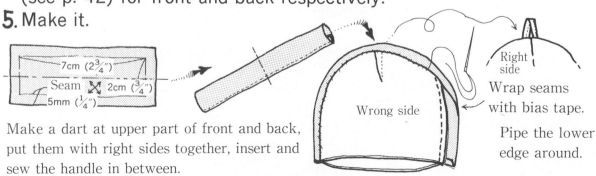

7cm (2¾″)
Seam
2cm (¾″)
5mm (¼″)

Make a dart at upper part of front and back, put them with right sides together, insert and sew the handle in between.

Wrong side

Right side
Wrap seams with bias tape.

Pipe the lower edge around.

30

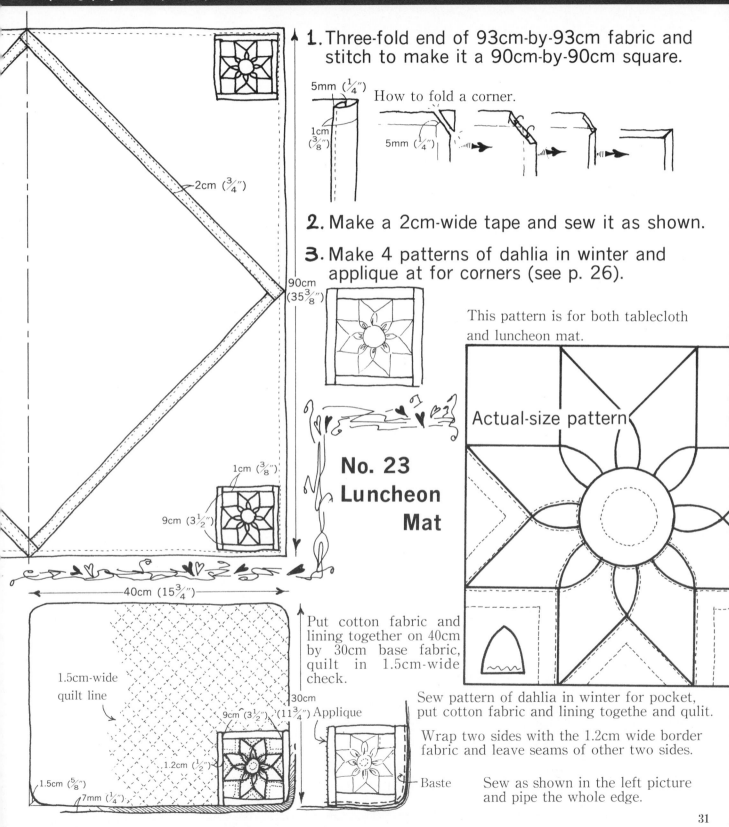

No. 22: white, 1m(39⅜″) by 1m(39⅜″); brown, 65cm(25½″) by 40cm(15¾″); fabric for patterns, a little
No. 23: fabric for patterns, a little; brown, 60cm(23⅝″) by 60cm(23⅝″); cotton fabric and fabric for lining, 50cm(19⅝″) by 45cm(17½″) each

1. Three-fold end of 93cm-by-93cm fabric and stitch to make it a 90cm-by-90cm square.

5mm (¼″)

How to fold a corner.

1cm (⅜″)

5mm (¼″)

2. Make a 2cm-wide tape and sew it as shown.

3. Make 4 patterns of dahlia in winter and applique at for corners (see p. 26).

2cm (¾″)

90cm (35⅜″)

1cm (⅜″)

9cm (3½″)

This pattern is for both tablecloth and luncheon mat.

Actual-size pattern

No. 23 Luncheon Mat

40cm (15¾″)

1.5cm-wide quilt line

9cm (3½″)

30cm (11¾″) Applique

1.2cm (½″)

1.5cm (⅝″)

7mm (¼″)

Put cotton fabric and lining together on 40cm by 30cm base fabric, quilt in 1.5cm-wide check.

Sew pattern of dahlia in winter for pocket, put cotton fabric and lining togethe and qulit.

Wrap two sides with the 1.2cm wide border fabric and leave seams of other two sides.

Baste

Sew as shown in the left picture and pipe the whole edge.

31

Fancy Dahlia in Winter

NO.24

The dahlia in winter highlights each of these organdy bags.
They are dramatic, fantasic, and wonderful.

Instructions on page 84.

NO.25

NO.26

Heart Keepsakes

Miniature heart cushions and frame bring sweet thoughts and feelings.
Girls love such cute things.
How about putting a favorite photo in the frame?

NO.27

NO.28

NO.29

**Insthuctions
on page 35.**

Materials No. 25: fabric (golden brown), 1m(39⅜″) by 40cm(15¾″); fabric for patterns, a little bit; cotton fabric, 50cm(19⅝″) by 30cm(11¾″); organdy (white), 60cm(23⅝″) by 70cm(27⅝″); (other colors), 60cm(23⅝″) by 60cm(23⅝″) each; core, 50cm(19⅝″) by 50cm(19⅝″), Nos. 24, 26: fabric for patterns, a little; organdy (White), 1m(39⅜″) by 1m(39⅜″); (other colors), 50cm(19⅝″) by 50cm(19⅝″) each; cotton fabric and core, 10cm(4″) by 10cm(4″) each; 3.5cm(1⅜″)-wide tape, 70cm(27⅝″); string, 2cm(¾″); beads and laces, a little

Fancy Dahlia in Winter p. 32

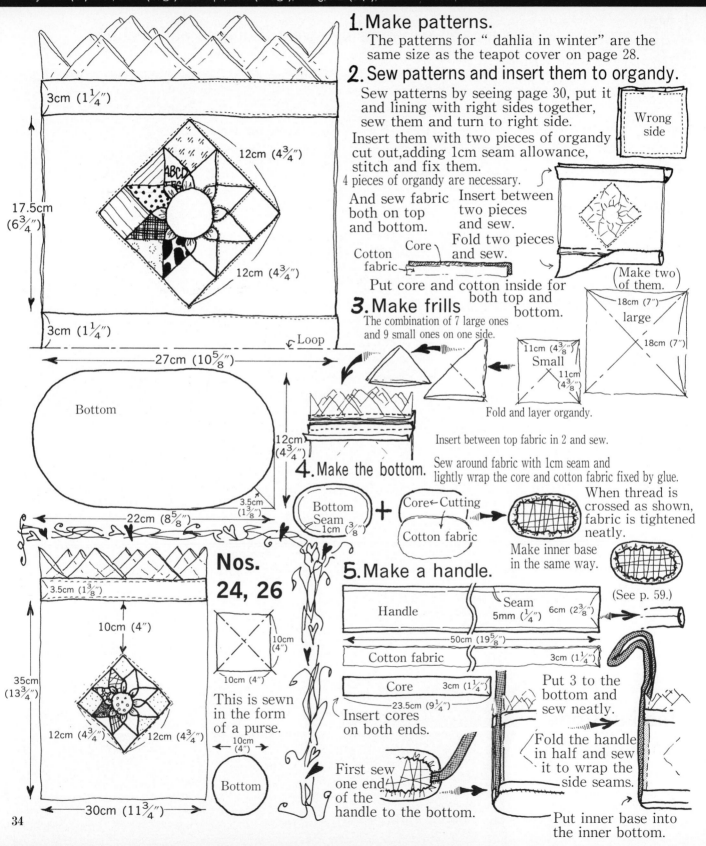

1. Make patterns.

The patterns for " dahlia in winter" are the same size as the teapot cover on page 28.

2. Sew patterns and insert them to organdy.

Sew patterns by seeing page 30, put it and lining with right sides together, sew them and turn to right side.

Insert them with two pieces of organdy cut out, adding 1cm seam allowance, stitch and fix them.

4 pieces of organdy are necessary.

And sew fabric both on top and bottom.

Insert between two pieces and sew.

Fold two pieces and sew.

Cotton fabric Core

Put core and cotton inside for both top and bottom.

Wrong side

(Make two of them.)

3. Make frills

The combination of 7 large ones and 9 small ones on one side.

18cm (7″) large 18cm (7″)

11cm (4⅜″) Small 11cm (4⅜″)

Fold and layer organdy.

Insert between top fabric in 2 and sew.

4. Make the bottom.

Sew around fabric with 1cm seam and lightly wrap the core and cotton fabric fixed by glue.

Bottom Seam 1cm (⅜″) + Core ← Cutting Cotton fabric

When thread is crossed as shown, fabric is tightened neatly.

Make inner base in the same way.

(See p. 59.)

5. Make a handle.

Handle Seam 5mm (¼″) 6cm (2⅜″)

50cm (19⅝″)

Cotton fabric 3cm (1¼″)

Core 3cm (1¼″)

23.5cm (9¼″)

Insert cores on both ends.

First sew one end of the handle to the bottom.

Put 3 to the bottom and sew neatly.

Fold the handle in half and sew it to wrap the side seams.

Put inner base into the inner bottom.

3cm (1¼″)

17.5cm (6¾″)

12cm (4¾″)

12cm (4¾″)

3cm (1¼″)

ABCD

Loop

27cm (10⅝″)

Bottom

12cm (4¾″)

3.5cm (1⅜″)

22cm (8⅝″)

Nos. 24, 26

3.5cm (1⅜″)

10cm (4″)

10cm (4″)

10cm (4″)

35cm (13¾″)

12cm (4¾″) 12cm (4¾″)

30cm (11¾″)

This is sewn in the form of a purse.

10cm (4″)

Bottom

Materials Nos. 27, 28: fabric for patterns, a little; cotton fabric, fabric for lining and back, 30cm(11¾″) by 30cm(11¾″) each; No. 25 embroidery thread, a little; synthetic cotton, proper quantity; laces, ribbons, and beads,a little; 5cm(2″)-wide lace, 1m70cm(67″) for No. 27, 3.5cm(1⅜″)-wide lace, 2m(80″) for No. 28   No. 29: fabric for patterns, a little bit; cotton fabric, 50cm(19⅝″) by 25cm(10″); back, 25cm(10″) by 25cm(10″); illustration board, 50cm(19⅝″) by 25cm(10″)

Heart Keepsakes   p. 33

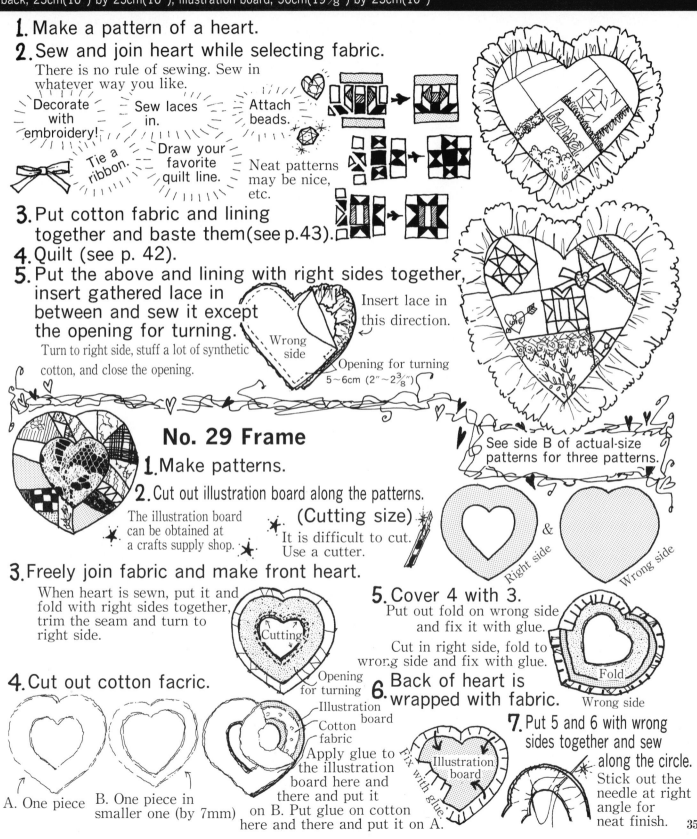

1. Make a pattern of a heart.

2. Sew and join heart while selecting fabric.

There is no rule of sewing. Sew in whatever way you like.

Decorate with embroidery!

Sew laces in.

Attach beads.

Tie a ribbon.

Draw your favorite quilt line.

Neat patterns may be nice, etc.

3. Put cotton fabric and lining together and baste them(see p.43).

4. Quilt (see p. 42).

5. Put the above and lining with right sides together, insert gathered lace in between and sew it except the opening for turning.

Turn to right side, stuff a lot of synthetic cotton, and close the opening.

Wrong side

Insert lace in this direction.

Opening for turning 5~6cm (2″~2⅜″)

No. 29 Frame

1. Make patterns.

2. Cut out illustration board along the patterns.

The illustration board can be obtained at a crafts supply shop.

(Cutting size)

It is difficult to cut. Use a cutter.

See side B of actual-size patterns for three patterns.

Right side   &   Wrong side

3. Freely join fabric and make front heart.

When heart is sewn, put it and fold with right sides together, trim the seam and turn to right side.

Cutting

Opening for turning

Illustration board

Cotton fabric

Apply glue to the illustration board here and there and put it on B. Put glue on cotton here and there and put it on A.

4. Cut out cotton facric.

A. One piece

B. One piece in smaller one (by 7mm)

5. Cover 4 with 3.

Put out fold on wrong side and fix it with glue.

Cut in right side, fold to wrong side and fix with glue.

Fold

Wrong side

6. Back of heart is wrapped with fabric.

Illustration board

Fix with glue

7. Put 5 and 6 with wrong sides together and sew along the circle.

Stick out the needle at right angle for neat finish.

35

Flower Frame (L, M, S)

NO.30

Quilted flowers made by bias. Create unique little solid figures. What scent do you think these flowers have? How about giving them as a birthday present? Or are they too gorgeous for that?

Instructions on page 38.

NO.31

NO.32

Make a Clock with Piece Work

Make an original handmade clock by placing clock parts into one piece. The name of the pattern is the wheel of fate. A meaningful little clock, isn't it?

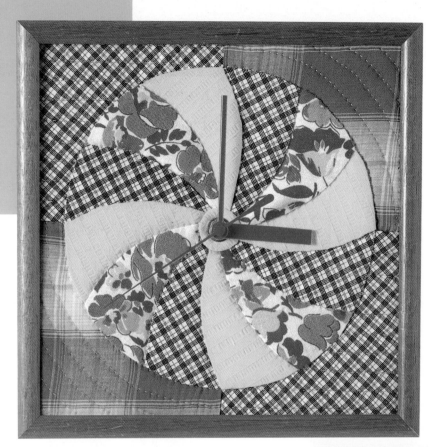

NO.33

Instructions on page 39.

NO.35

NO.34

Materials   No. 30: fabric for patterns, a little; dark brown cotton fabric and fabric for lining, 30cm(11¾") by 30cm(11¾") each; frame   No. 31: whitish fabric, cotton fabric and fabric for lining, 25cm(10") by 25cm(10") each; fabric for patterns, a little; 4cm(1⅝")-wide ribbon, 50cm(19⅝"); frame   No. 32: fabric for patterns, a little; whitish fabric, cotton fabric and fabric for lining, 50cm(19⅝") by 50cm(19⅝") each; frame

Flower Frame (L, M, S)   p. 36

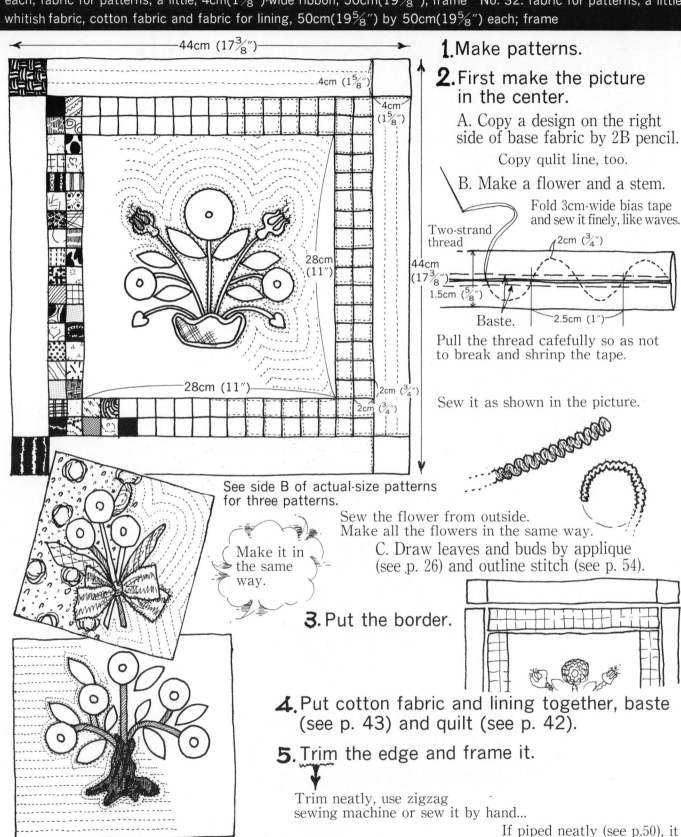

44cm (17⅜")

4cm (1⅝")

4cm (1⅝")

28cm (11")

28cm (11")

2cm (¾")

2cm (¾")

See side B of actual-size patterns for three patterns.

Make it in the same way.

1. Make patterns.

2. First make the picture in the center.

A. Copy a design on the right side of base fabric by 2B pencil.

Copy qulit line, too.

B. Make a flower and a stem.

Fold 3cm-wide bias tape and sew it finely, like waves.

Two-strand thread

2cm (¾")

44cm (17⅜")

1.5cm (⅝")

Baste.

2.5cm (1")

Pull the thread cafefully so as not to break and shrinp the tape.

Sew it as shown in the picture.

Sew the flower from outside.
Make all the flowers in the same way.

C. Draw leaves and buds by applique (see p. 26) and outline stitch (see p. 54).

3. Put the border.

4. Put cotton fabric and lining together, baste (see p. 43) and quilt (see p. 42).

5. Trim the edge and frame it.

Trim neatly, use zigzag sewing machine or sew it by hand...

If piped neatly (see p.50), it can be decorated as is.

Materials Nos. 33, 34: fabric for patterns, a little; cotton fabric and fabric for lining, 30cm(11¾″) by 30cm(11¾″) each; clock parts; frame No. 35: fabric for patterns, a little; cotton fabric and fabric for lining, 20cm(7¾″) by 20cm(7¾″) each; clock parts, frame

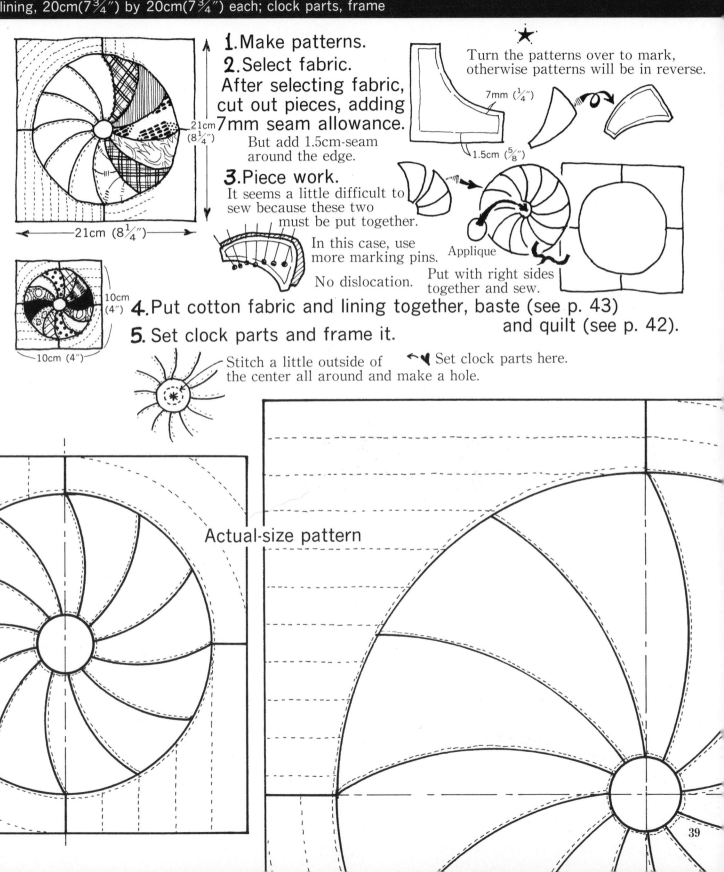

21cm (8¼″)

21cm (8¼″)

10cm (4″)

10cm (4″)

1. Make patterns.

2. Select fabric.
After selecting fabric, cut out pieces, adding 7mm seam allowance.
But add 1.5cm-seam around the edge.

3. Piece work.
It seems a little difficult to sew because these two must be put together.

In this case, use more marking pins.

No dislocation.

★ Turn the patterns over to mark, otherwise patterns will be in reverse.

7mm (¼″)

1.5cm (⅝″)

7mm (¼″)

Applique

Put with right sides together and sew.

4. Put cotton fabric and lining together, baste (see p. 43) and quilt (see p. 42).

5. Set clock parts and frame it.

Stitch a little outside of the center all around and make a hole.

Set clock parts here.

Actual-size pattern

Tablecloth
and
Matching Pillows

Long chats around the table are so cozy at night. Look at the colors and patterns of the square parts. The vivid colors really stand out against the muted backgrounds, especially on the pillows.

NO.37

NO.36

Instructions on pages 42 and 43.

NO.38

Materials

No. 36: blackish fabric, 2m20cm(86½") by 1m(39⅜"); fabric for patterns, a little; cotton fabric and fabric for lining, 2m20cm(86½") by 2m20cm(86½") each.

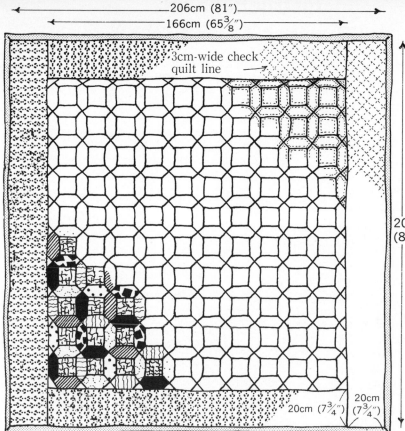

←—————206cm (81")—————→
←————166cm (65⅜")————→

3cm-wide check
quilt line

206cm
(81")

20cm (7¾") 20cm (7¾")

See side B of actual-size pattern.

1. Make patterns.

2. Select your fabric carefully.
   ★ Pay careful attention to each piece.
   After selecting fabric, cut out pieces, adding 7mm seam allowance.

3. Piece work.

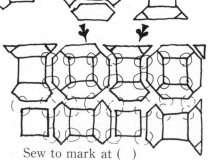

Sew to mark at ( )

4. Put cotton fabric and lining together and baste them (see p. 43)

5. Quilt (see p. 42).

6. Pipe around the edge (see p. 50).

How to quilt

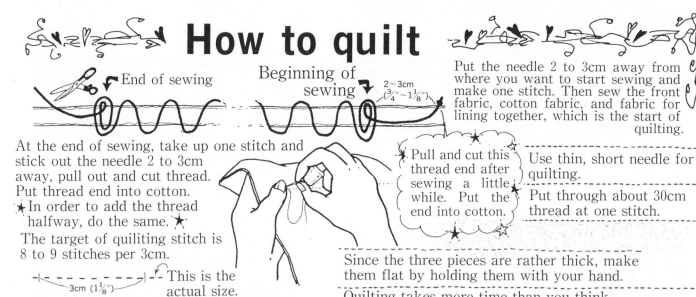

End of sewing

Beginning of sewing

2~3cm
(¾"~1⅛")

Put the needle 2 to 3cm away from where you want to start sewing and make one stitch. Then sew the front fabric, cotton fabric, and fabric for lining together, which is the start of quilting.

At the end of sewing, take up one stitch and stick out the needle 2 to 3cm away, pull out and cut thread. Put thread end into cotton.
★ In order to add the thread halfway, do the same. ★
The target of quilting stitch is 8 to 9 stitches per 3cm.

←———3cm (1⅛")———→ This is the actual size.

However, it is only a target. Even if your stitch is larger, it shows your unique style
Do not mind at all!

★ Pull and cut this thread end after sewing a little while. Put the end into cotton.

Use thin, short needle for quilting.

Put through about 30cm thread at one stitch.

Since the three pieces are rather thick, make them flat by holding them with your hand.

Quilting takes more time than you think.

Be patient and take it easy. The art of quilting is to get used to it.
Good luck.

Nos. 37, 38: yellowish brown, 40cm(15¾") by 40cm(15¾") each; black, 1m(39⅜") by 1m(39⅜"); black stripe, 50cm(19⅝") by 50cm(19⅝"); fabric for patterns, a little; cotton fabric and fabric for lining, 70cm(27⅝") by 70cm(27⅝") each; 50cm(19⅝") zipper; yarn, a little

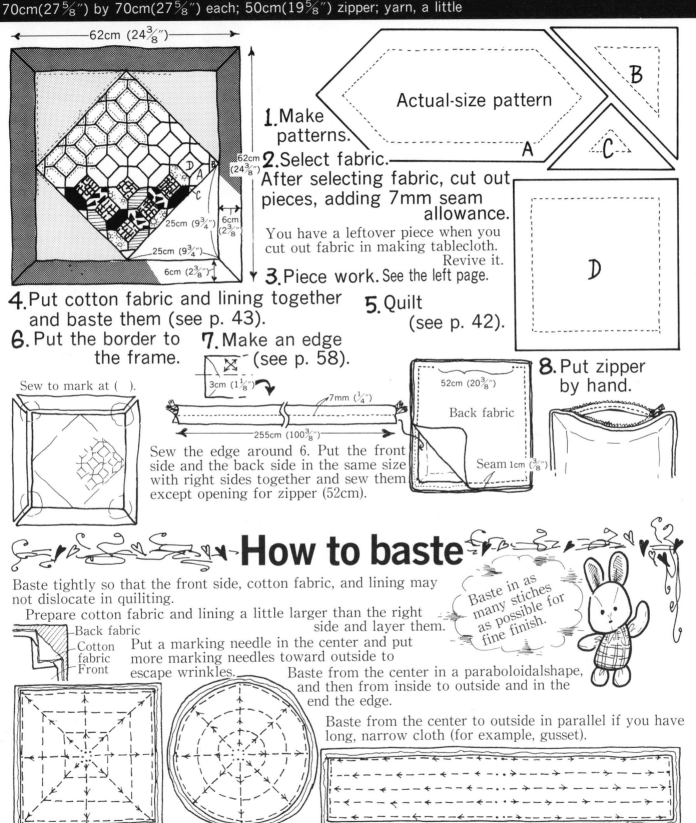

62cm (24³⁄₈")

62cm (24³⁄₈")

Actual-size pattern

A B C D

1. Make patterns.

2. Select fabric.
After selecting fabric, cut out pieces, adding 7mm seam allowance.

You have a leftover piece when you cut out fabric in making tablecloth. Revive it.

3. Piece work. See the left page.

4. Put cotton fabric and lining together and baste them (see p. 43).

5. Quilt (see p. 42).

6. Put the border to the frame.

7. Make an edge (see p. 58).

8. Put zipper by hand.

25cm (9¾") 6cm (2³⁄₈")
25cm (9¾")
6cm (2³⁄₈")

Sew to mark at ( ).

3cm (1⅛") 7mm (¼")
255cm (100³⁄₈")

52cm (20³⁄₈")
Back fabric
Seam 1cm (³⁄₈")

Sew the edge around 6. Put the front side and the back side in the same size with right sides together and sew them except opening for zipper (52cm).

How to baste

Baste tightly so that the front side, cotton fabric, and lining may not dislocate in quilting.

Prepare cotton fabric and lining a little larger than the right side and layer them.

Put a marking needle in the center and put more marking needles toward outside to escape wrinkles.

Baste in as many stiches as possible for fine finish.

Back fabric
Cotton fabric
Front

Baste from the center in a paraboloidalshape, and then from inside to outside and in the end the edge.

Baste from the center to outside in parallel if you have long, narrow cloth (for example, gusset).

Variations of Fluffy Puff

NO.39

A large magazine rack, a circular bag,
and a basket-type bag. They conveniently hold such
everyday item's as newspapers, magazines, sewing tools,
cosmetics, and jewelry.

NO.40

**Instructions
on page 46.**

NO.41

Variation of Hexagon Part 1

A larger one is used for a newspaper rack. The pot cover has a patchwork of one row of flowers. You can use them as you like.

NO.42

Instructions on page 47.

NO.43

Materials   No. 39: fabric for patterns, a little; base fabric, 50cm(19⅝″) square; cotton fabric, fabric for lining, 40cm(15¾″) by 25cm(10″) each; inner bag, 50cm(19⅝″) by 30cm(11¾″); 45cm(17⅝″) zipper; cardboard, 20cm(7¾″) by 15cm(6″)   No. 40: fabric for patterns, a little; black (inluding inner bag); 1m(39⅜″) square; cotton fabric, fabric for lining, 1m(39⅜″) by 30cm(11¾″) each; magazine rack frame   No. 41: white, 1m50cm(59″) by 1m(39⅜″); fabric for patterns, a little; base fabric, 70cm(27⅝″) square; cotton fabric 60cm(23⅝″) by 40cm(15¾″); fabric for lining, illustration board, 40cm(15¾″) by 30cm(11¾″) each; inner bag, 1m50cm(59″) by 25cm(10″); synthetic cotton, proper quantity

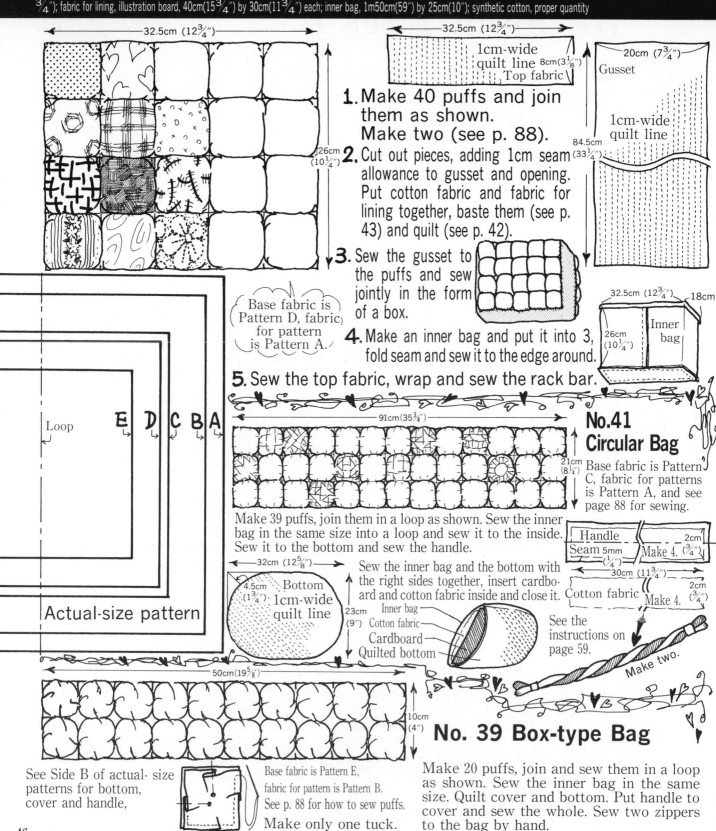

1. Make 40 puffs and join them as shown.
Make two (see p. 88).

2. Cut out pieces, adding 1cm seam allowance to gusset and opening. Put cotton fabric and fabric for lining together, baste them (see p. 43) and quilt (see p. 42).

3. Sew the gusset to the puffs and sew jointly in the form of a box.

Base fabric is Pattern D, fabric for pattern is Pattern A.

4. Make an inner bag and put it into 3, fold seam and sew it to the edge around.

5. Sew the top fabric, wrap and sew the rack bar.

32.5cm (12¾″)
1cm-wide quilt line
8cm(3⅛″)
Top fabric

20cm (7¾″)
Gusset
1cm-wide quilt line
84.5cm (33¼″)

32.5cm (12¾″)   18cm
26cm (10¼″)
Inner bag

No.41 Circular Bag
Base fabric is Pattern C, fabric for patterns is Pattern A, and see page 88 for sewing.

91cm(35¾″)
21cm (8¼″)

Make 39 puffs, join them in a loop as shown. Sew the inner bag in the same size into a loop and sew it to the inside. Sew it to the bottom and sew the handle.

Loop   E D C B A

Actual-size pattern

32cm (12⅝″)
4.5cm (1¾″)
Bottom
1cm-wide quilt line
23cm (9″)

Inner bag
Cotton fabric
Cardboard
Quilted bottom

Sew the inner bag and the bottom with the right sides together, insert cardboard and cotton fabric inside and close it.

Handle   2cm (¾″)
Seam 5mm (¼″)   Make 4.
30cm (11¾″)
Cotton fabric   Make 4.   2cm (¾″)

See the instructions on page 59.

Make two.

50cm(19⅝″)
10cm (4″)

No. 39 Box-type Bag

See Side B of actual-size patterns for bottom, cover and handle,

Base fabric is Pattern E, fabric for pattern is Pattern B. See p. 88 for how to sew puffs. Make only one tuck.

Make 20 puffs, join and sew them in a loop as shown. Sew the inner bag in the same size. Quilt cover and bottom. Put handle to cover and sew the whole. Sew two zippers to the bag by hand.

Variation of Hexagon Part 1   p. 45

Materials

No. 42: Fabric for patterns, a little; cotton fabric, fabric for lining, 75cm(29⅝″) by 20cm(7¾″) each

No. 43: Fabric for patterns, a little; cotton fabric, fabric for lining, 1m30cm(51⅛″) by 30cm(11¾″) each

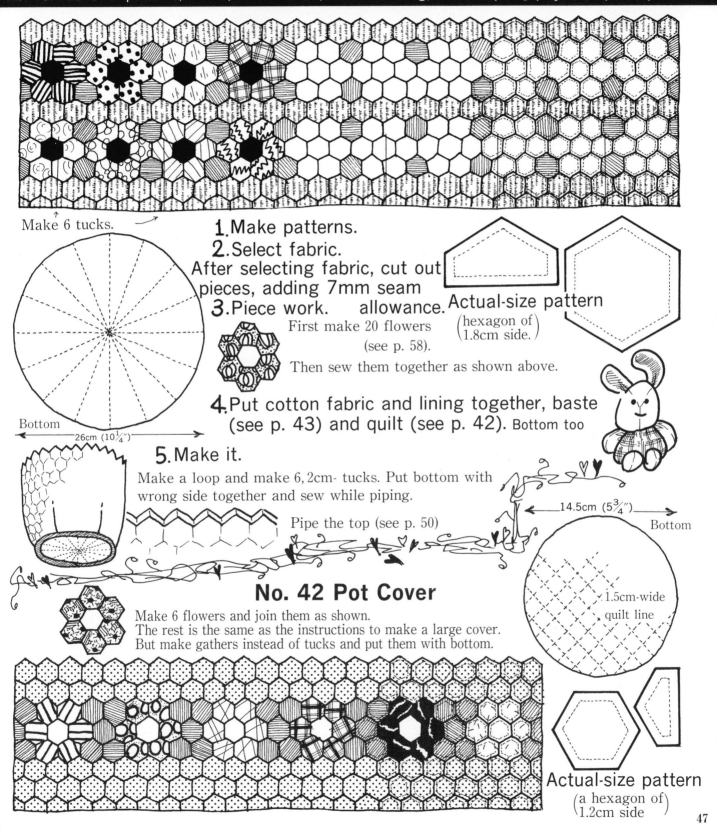

Make 6 tucks.

1. Make patterns.
2. Select fabric.

After selecting fabric, cut out pieces, adding 7mm seam

3. Piece work.   allowance.

First make 20 flowers (see p. 58).

Then sew them together as shown above.

Actual-size pattern
(hexagon of)
(1.8cm side.)

4. Put cotton fabric and lining together, baste (see p. 43) and quilt (see p. 42). Bottom too

5. Make it.

Make a loop and make 6, 2cm- tucks. Put bottom with wrong side together and sew while piping.

Pipe the top (see p. 50)

Bottom

26cm (10¼″)

14.5cm (5¾″)

Bottom

1.5cm-wide quilt line

No. 42 Pot Cover

Make 6 flowers and join them as shown.
The rest is the same as the instructions to make a large cover.
But make gathers instead of tucks and put them with bottom.

Actual-size pattern
(a hexagon of)
(1.2cm side)

47

NO.44

Uncle Tom

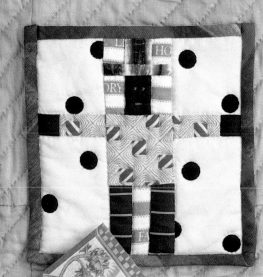

Children's Favorite Time-Teatime

Uncle Tom's wall pocket is for the children's room. The luncheon mat in the shape of a house and the basket cover with houses are put on the table when the children are good. Today golden baked bread and sweet cocoa are served at teatime.

NO.45

NO.46

NO.47

NO.48

**Instructions
on pages 50 and 51.**

Materials   No. 44: Fabric for patterns, a little; cotton fabric, fabric for lining, 80cm(31⅜″) by 70cm(27⅝″), No. 25 embroidery thread, a little; 60cm(23⅝″) string; 4.5cm(1¾″)-wide ribbon; 45cm(17⅝″) bar

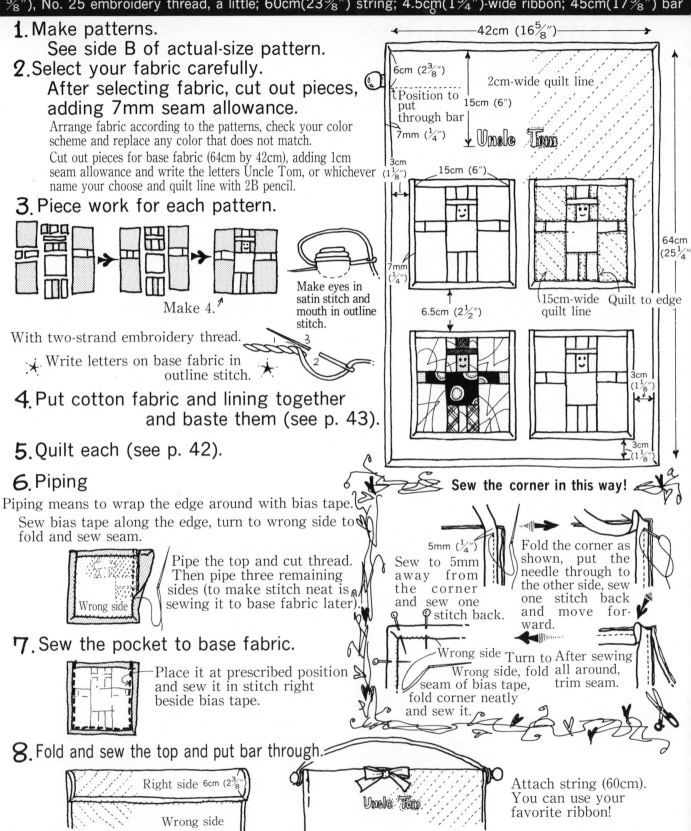

1. Make patterns.
   See side B of actual-size pattern.

2. Select your fabric carefully.
   After selecting fabric, cut out pieces, adding 7mm seam allowance.

Arrange fabric according to the patterns, check your color scheme and replace any color that does not match.

Cut out pieces for base fabric (64cm by 42cm), adding 1cm seam allowance and write the letters Uncle Tom, or whichever name your choose and quilt line with 2B pencil.

3. Piece work for each pattern.

Make 4.

With two-strand embroidery thread.

Make eyes in satin stitch and mouth in outline stitch.

⚹ Write letters on base fabric in outline stitch. ⚹

4. Put cotton fabric and lining together and baste them (see p. 43).

5. Quilt each (see p. 42).

6. Piping

Piping means to wrap the edge around with bias tape.
Sew bias tape along the edge, turn to wrong side to fold and sew seam.

Wrong side

Pipe the top and cut thread. Then pipe three remaining sides (to make stitch neat is sewing it to base fabric later).

7. Sew the pocket to base fabric.

Place it at prescribed position and sew it in stitch right beside bias tape.

8. Fold and sew the top and put bar through.

Right side 6cm (2⅜″)

Wrong side

Sew the corner in this way!

5mm (¼″)
Sew to 5mm away from the corner and sew one stitch back.

Fold the corner as shown, put the needle through to the other side, sew one stitch back and move forward.

Wrong side Turn to After sewing
Wrong side, fold all around,
seam of bias tape, trim seam.
fold corner neatly
and sew it.

Uncle Tom

Attach string (60cm). You can use your favorite ribbon!

— labels within diagram —
42cm (16⅝″)
6cm (2⅜″)
2cm-wide quilt line
Position to put through bar
15cm (6″)
7mm (¼″)
Uncle Tom
3cm (1⅛″)
15cm (6″)
64cm (25¼″)
7mm (¼″)
6.5cm (2½″)
15cm-wide Quilt to edge quilt line
3cm (1⅛″)
3cm (1⅛″)

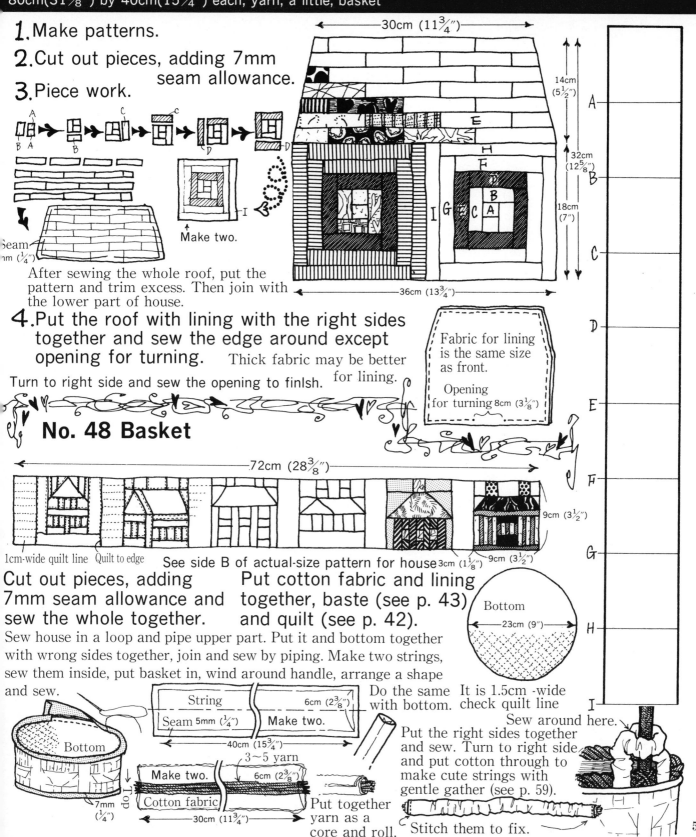

Nos. 45. 46: fabric for patterns, a little; fabric for lining, 45cm(17⅝″) by 40cm(15¾″)
No. 46: white, 60cm(23⅝″) by 50cm(19⅝″); fabric for patterns, a little; cotton fabric, fabric for lining, 80cm(31⅜″) by 40cm(15¾″) each; yarn, a little; basket

1. Make patterns.
2. Cut out pieces, adding 7mm seam allowance.
3. Piece work.

30cm (11¾″)

14cm (5½″)
A

32cm (12⅝″)
B

18cm (7″)
C

E

H
F
D
B
A
I G Z C A

36cm (13¾″)

Make two.

Seam
mm (¼″)

After sewing the whole roof, put the pattern and trim excess. Then join with the lower part of house.

4. Put the roof with lining with the right sides together and sew the edge around except opening for turning. Thick fabric may be better for lining.

Turn to right side and sew the opening to finish.

Fabric for lining is the same size as front.

Opening for turning 8cm (3⅛″)

D

E

No. 48 Basket

72cm (28⅜″)

F

9cm (3½″)

G

1cm-wide quilt line   Quilt to edge   See side B of actual-size pattern for house 3cm (1⅛″)   9cm (3½″)

Cut out pieces, adding 7mm seam allowance and sew the whole together.

Put cotton fabric and lining together, baste (see p. 43) and quilt (see p. 42).

Bottom
23cm (9″)

H

Sew house in a loop and pipe upper part. Put it and bottom together with wrong sides together, join and sew by piping. Make two strings, sew them inside, put basket in, wind around handle, arrange a shape and sew.

Do the same with bottom. It is 1.5cm -wide check quilt line

Sew around here.

Put the right sides together and sew. Turn to right side and put cotton through to make cute strings with gentle gather (see p. 59).

I

String   6cm (2⅜″)
Seam 5mm (¼″)   Make two.
40cm (15¾″)

3～5 yarn

Make two.   6cm (2⅜″)
Cotton fabric
30cm (11¾″)

Bottom

7mm (¼″)
Top

Put together yarn as a core and roll.

Stitch them to fix.

51

Fairy Tales Fantasy

Don't they make a nice wedding present? They look well with a teapot in a solid color and large teacups. The message is "I'm sure you'll create a sweet home!" Such a fresh and pleasant was to start every morning.

NO.49

Instructions
on pages 54 and 55.

Fairy Tales Fantasy   pp. 52, 53

Materials

Nos. 49, 50: white, cotton fabric, fabric for lining, 40cm(15¾″) by 50cm(19⅝″) each; fabric for patterns, a little; No. 25 embroidery thread, a little

1. Make patterns.

2. Draw pictures on base fabric with fabric or thread, etc.

Applique and embroider according to design (see p. 26).

It might be nice to use different fabric. for example, basket pattern fabric for basket, grain pattern for wooden fence, and letter-printed fabric for books and newspapers...

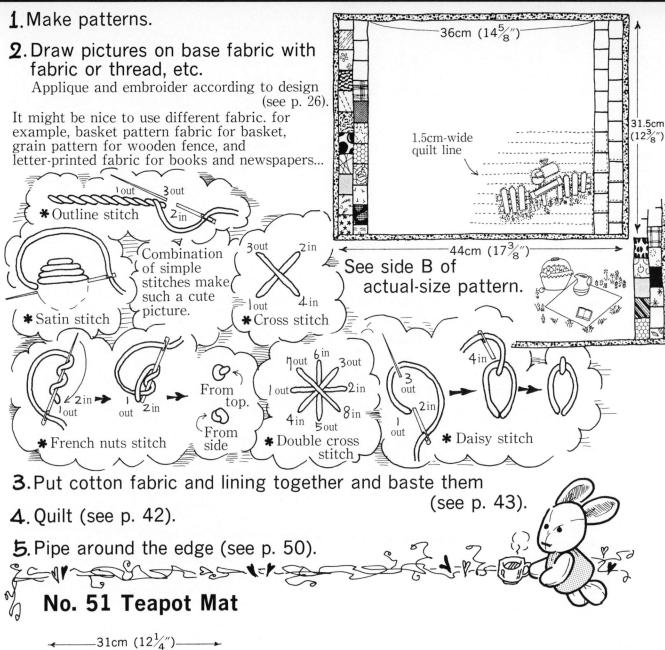

36cm (14⅝″)

31.5cm (12⅜″)

1.5cm-wide quilt line

44cm (17⅜″)

See side B of actual-size pattern.

* Outline stitch

1 out   3 out   2 in

Combination of simple stitches make such a cute picture.

* Satin stitch

* Cross stitch
3 out   2 in   1 out   4 in

* French nuts stitch
1 out   2 in   out   2 in

From top.   From side

* Double cross stitch
7 out   6 in   3 out   1 out   2 in   4 in   8 in   5 out

* Daisy stitch
3 out   2 in   1 out   4 in

3. Put cotton fabric and lining together and baste them (see p. 43).

4. Quilt (see p. 42).

5. Pipe around the edge (see p. 50).

No. 51 Teapot Mat

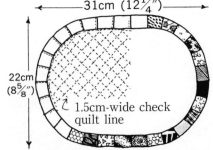

31cm (12¼″)

22cm (8⅝″)

1.5cm-wide check quilt line

Cut out pieces, adding 7mm seam allowance, sew them together and draw quilt line on right side of fabric with 2B pencil. Add 7mm seam allowance, put lining with right sides together, sew them, put cotton fabric, turn to right side, close opening and baste (see p. 43).

Quilt carefully to finish (see p. 42).

See side B of actual-size pattern.

54

No. 51: white, 60cm(23⅝″) by 30cm(11¾″); fabric for patterns, a little; cotton fabric, fabric for lining, 50cm(19⅝″) by 50cm(19⅝″) each; No. 25 embroidery thread

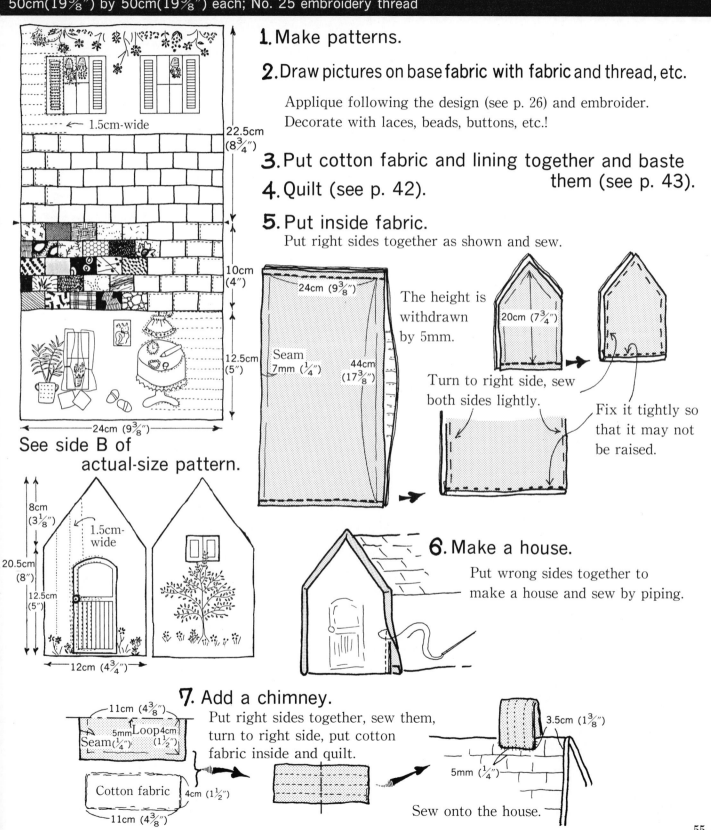

1. Make patterns.

2. Draw pictures on base fabric with fabric and thread, etc.

Applique following the design (see p. 26) and embroider. Decorate with laces, beads, buttons, etc.!

3. Put cotton fabric and lining together and baste them (see p. 43).

4. Quilt (see p. 42).

5. Put inside fabric.

Put right sides together as shown and sew.

The height is withdrawn by 5mm.

Turn to right side, sew both sides lightly.

Fix it tightly so that it may not be raised.

1.5cm-wide

22.5cm (8¾″)

10cm (4″)

12.5cm (5″)

24cm (9⅜″)

See side B of actual-size pattern.

8cm (3⅛″)

1.5cm-wide

20.5cm (8″)

12.5cm (5″)

12cm (4¾″)

24cm (9⅜″)

Seam 7mm (¼″)

44cm (17⅜″)

20cm (7¾″)

6. Make a house.

Put wrong sides together to make a house and sew by piping.

7. Add a chimney.

Put right sides together, sew them, turn to right side, put cotton fabric inside and quilt.

11cm (4⅜″)

5mm Loop 4cm
Seam (¼″) (1½″)

Cotton fabric

4cm (1½″)

11cm (4⅜″)

3.5cm (1⅜″)

5mm (¼″)

Sew onto the house.

55

Three Kinds of Electric Cooker Covers and Pot Holder

NO.52

Nice kitchen accessories of coffee cup, hexagon, diamond-shaped log cabin. Make patchwork according to the shape of your electric cooker. Keeping food warm helps to guarantee it nutrition.

NO.53

NO.54

NO.55

NO.56

**Instructions
on pages 58 and 59.**

Three kinds of electric cooker covers and pot holder pp.56,57

Materials   No. 52: fabric for patterns, a little; cotton fabric, fabric for lining, 1m20cm(47⅛") by 40cm(15¾") each;   No. 53: fabric for patterns, a little; silver, 40cm(15¾") by 40cm(15¾"); black, 50cm(19⅝") by 50cm(19⅝"); cotton fabric, fabric for lining, 1m20cm(47⅛") by 30cm(11¾") each;   No. 54: towel fabric, 30cm(11¾") by 30cm(11¾"); fabric for patterns, a little

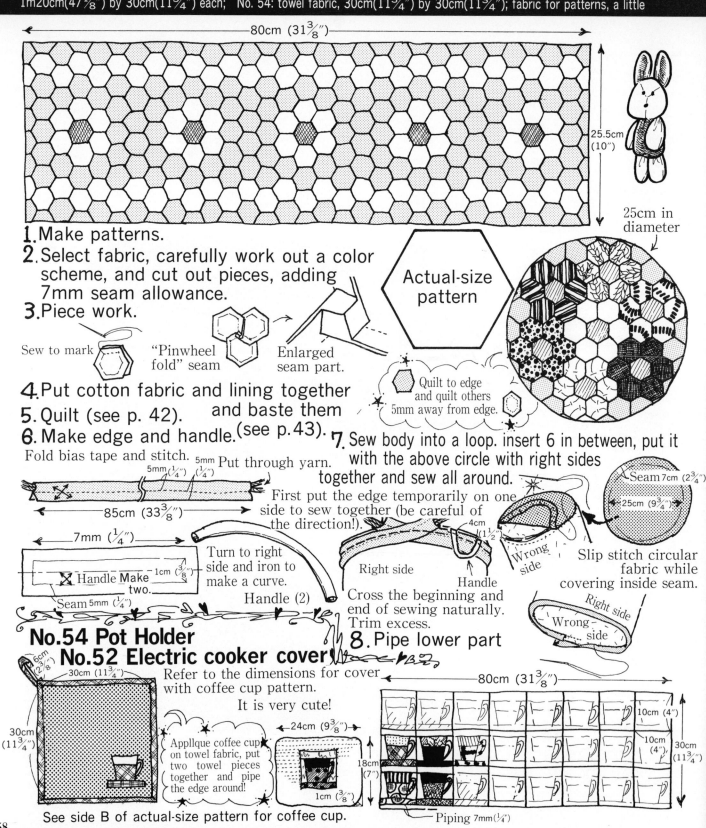

80cm (31⅜")

25.5cm (10")

25cm in diameter

1. Make patterns.

2. Select fabric, carefully work out a color scheme, and cut out pieces, adding 7mm seam allowance.

3. Piece work.

Sew to mark

"Pinwheel fold" seam

Enlarged seam part.

Actual-size pattern

Quilt to edge and quilt others 5mm away from edge.

4. Put cotton fabric and lining together and baste them (see p. 43).

5. Quilt (see p. 42).

6. Make edge and handle.

Fold bias tape and stitch.   5mm Put through yarn.

5mm(¼")   (¼")

85cm (33⅜")

7mm (¼")

Handle Make two.

Seam 5mm (¼")

Turn to right side and iron to make a curve.

Handle (2)

7. Sew body into a loop. insert 6 in between, put it with the above circle with right sides together and sew all around.

First put the edge temporarily on one side to sew together (be careful of the direction!).

Right side

4cm (1½")

Handle

Cross the beginning and end of sewing naturally. Trim excess.

Wrong side

Seam 7cm (2¾")

25cm (9¾")

Slip stitch circular fabric while covering inside seam.

Right side

Wrong side

8. Pipe lower part

No.54 Pot Holder
No.52 Electric cooker cover

6cm (2⅜")

30cm (11¾")

30cm (11¾")

Refer to the dimensions for cover with coffee cup pattern.

It is very cute!

Appllque coffee cup on towel fabric, put two towel pieces together and pipe the edge around!

24cm (9⅜")

18cm (7")

1cm (⅜")

80cm (31⅜")

10cm (4")

10cm (4")

30cm (11¾")

See side B of actual-size pattern for coffee cup.

Piping 7mm(¼")

Nos. 55, 56: fabric for patterns, a little; cotton fabric, fabric for lining 1m(39⅜″) by 40cm(15¾″) each; synthetic cotton, a little

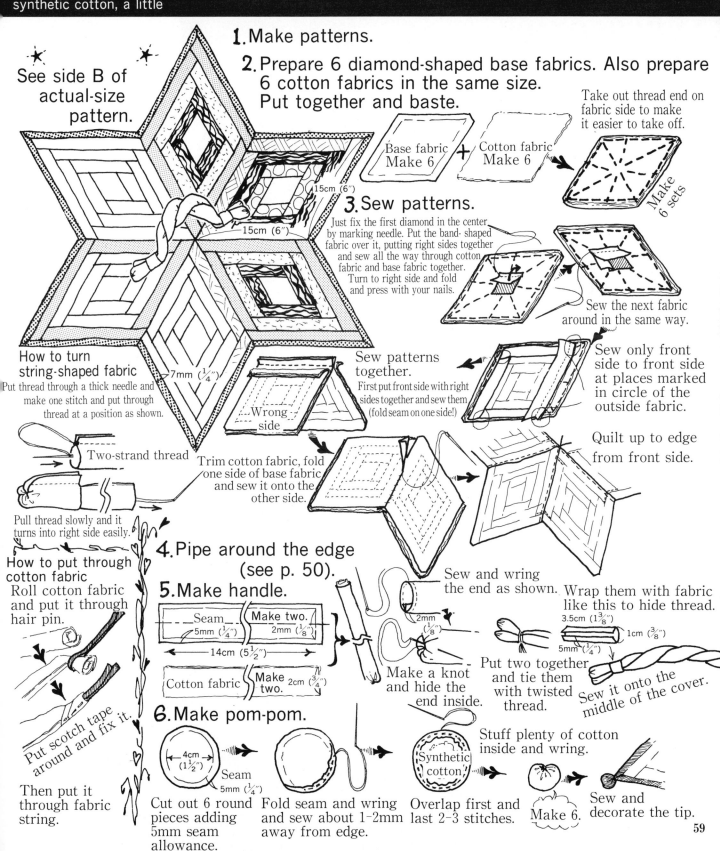

See side B of actual-size pattern.

1. Make patterns.

2. Prepare 6 diamond-shaped base fabrics. Also prepare 6 cotton fabrics in the same size. Put together and baste.

Base fabric Make 6 + Cotton fabric Make 6

Take out thread end on fabric side to make it easier to take off.

Make 6 sets

3. Sew patterns.

Just fix the first diamond in the center by marking needle. Put the band-shaped fabric over it, putting right sides together and sew all the way through cotton fabric and base fabric together. Turn to right side and fold and press with your nails.

15cm (6″)

15cm (6″)

7mm (¼″)

Sew the next fabric around in the same way.

Sew only front side to front side at places marked in circle of the outside fabric.

Quilt up to edge from front side.

How to turn string-shaped fabric

Put thread through a thick needle and make one stitch and put through thread at a position as shown.

Two-strand thread

Sew patterns together.

First put front side with right sides together and sew them (fold seam on one side!)

Wrong side

Trim cotton fabric, fold one side of base fabric and sew it onto the other side.

Pull thread slowly and it turns into right side easily.

How to put through cotton fabric

Roll cotton fabric and put it through hair pin.

4. Pipe around the edge (see p. 50).

5. Make handle.

Seam 5mm (¼″) Make two. 2mm (⅛″)

14cm (5½″)

Cotton fabric Make two. 2cm (¾″)

Sew and wring the end as shown.

2mm (⅛″)

Make a knot and hide the end inside.

Wrap them with fabric like this to hide thread.

3.5cm (1⅜″)

1cm (⅜″)

5mm (¼″)

Put two together and tie them with twisted thread.

Sew it onto the middle of the cover.

Put scotch tape around and fix it.

Then put it through fabric string.

6. Make pom-pom.

4cm (1½″)

Seam 5mm (¼″)

Cut out 6 round pieces adding 5mm seam allowance.

Fold seam and wring and sew about 1-2mm away from edge.

Synthetic cotton

Overlap first and last 2-3 stitches.

Stuff plenty of cotton inside and wring.

Make 6.

Sew and decorate the tip.

59

Nice Kitchen Accessories

*Hang puff wall pocket on the wall of housewife's corner.
*Use notebook holder and hook with magnet on the refrigerator.
*And rooster pot holder
They are all good friends in the kitchen.

NO.57

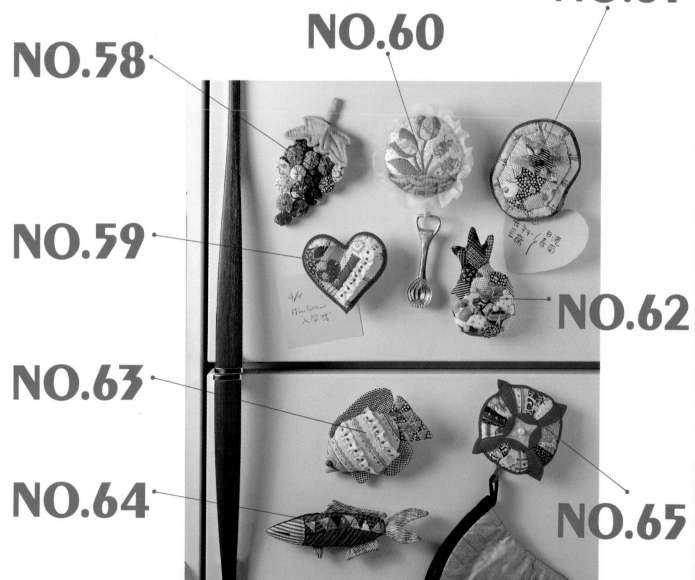

NO.58

NO.59

NO.60

NO.61

NO.62

NO.63

NO.64

NO.65

NO.67

Nice Kitchen Accessories   pp. 60, 61

Materials No. 57: fabric for patterns, a little; white, cotton fabric, fabric for lining, 40cm (15¾") square each; base fabric, 30cm(11¾") square; No. 25 embroidery thread, a little; 2cm(¾")-wide string, 55cm(21⅝"); 30cm(11¾") bar, synthetic cotton, proper quantity; metal fittings, 3;   No. 58: fabric for patterns, a little; organdy, 40cm(15¾"); cotton fabric, a little; synthetic cotton, proper quantity;   Nos. 59, 60-65: fabric for patterns, a little; cotton fabric, fabric for lining, a little each; synthetic cotton, proper quantity; beads; laces

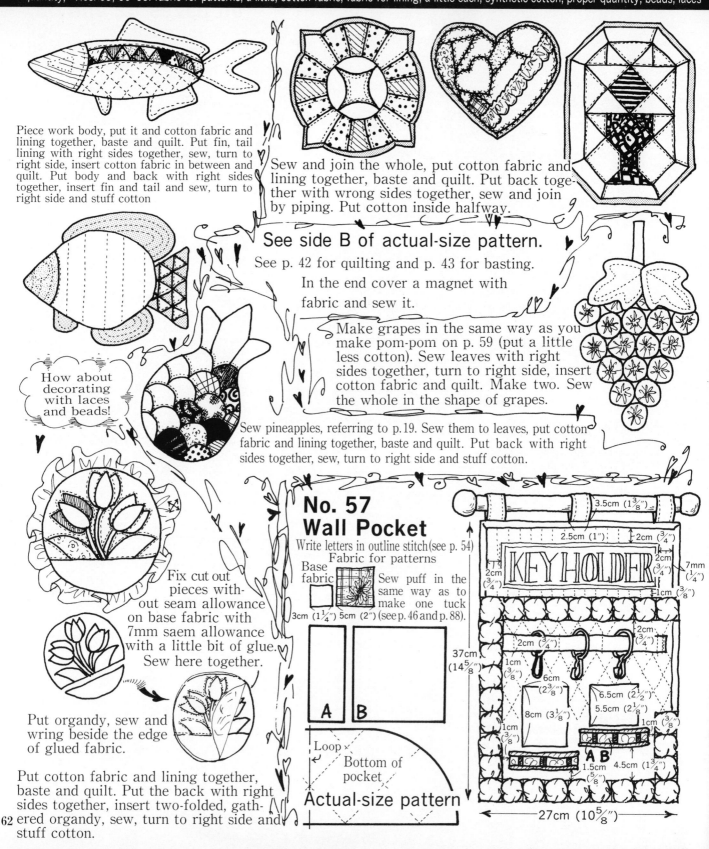

Piece work body, put it and cotton fabric and lining together, baste and quilt. Put fin, tail lining with right sides together, sew, turn to right side, insert cotton fabric in between and quilt. Put body and back with right sides together, insert fin and tail and sew, turn to right side and stuff cotton

Sew and join the whole, put cotton fabric and lining together, baste and quilt. Put back together with wrong sides together, sew and join by piping. Put cotton inside halfway.

See side B of actual-size pattern.

See p. 42 for quilting and p. 43 for basting.

In the end cover a magnet with fabric and sew it.

Make grapes in the same way as you make pom-pom on p. 59 (put a little less cotton). Sew leaves with right sides together, turn to right side, insert cotton fabric and quilt. Make two. Sew the whole in the shape of grapes.

How about decorating with laces and beads!

Sew pineapples, referring to p.19. Sew them to leaves, put cotton fabric and lining together, baste and quilt. Put back with right sides together, sew, turn to right side and stuff cotton.

Fix cut out pieces without seam allowance on base fabric with 7mm saem allowance with a little bit of glue. Sew here together.

Put organdy, sew and wring beside the edge of glued fabric.

Put cotton fabric and lining together, baste and quilt. Put the back with right sides together, insert two-folded, gathered organdy, sew, turn to right side and stuff cotton.

No. 57 Wall Pocket

Write letters in outline stitch(see p. 54)
Fabric for patterns

Base fabric

Sew puff in the same way as to make one tuck (see p. 46 and p. 88).

3cm (1¼") 5cm (2")

A   B

Loop
Bottom of pocket

Actual-size pattern

KEY HOLDER

3.5cm (1⅜")
2.5cm (1")
2cm (¾")
2cm (¾")
7mm (¼")
1cm (⅜")
2cm (¾")
2cm (¾")
1cm (⅜")
6cm (2⅜")
6.5cm (2½")
5.5cm (2⅛")
8cm (3⅛")
1cm (⅜")
1cm (⅜")
A B
1.5cm (⅝")
4.5cm (1¾")
37cm (14⅝")
← 27cm (10⅝") →

No. 60: fabric for patterns, a little; cotton fabric, fabric for lining, a little each; synthetic cotton, a little

Nos. 58–65: magnet for each   Nos. 66, 67: fabric for patterns, a little; cotton fabric, 35cm(13¾″) by 20cm(7¾″); fabric for lining, 20cm(7¾″) by 20cm(7¾″); 2 black beads; synthetic cotton

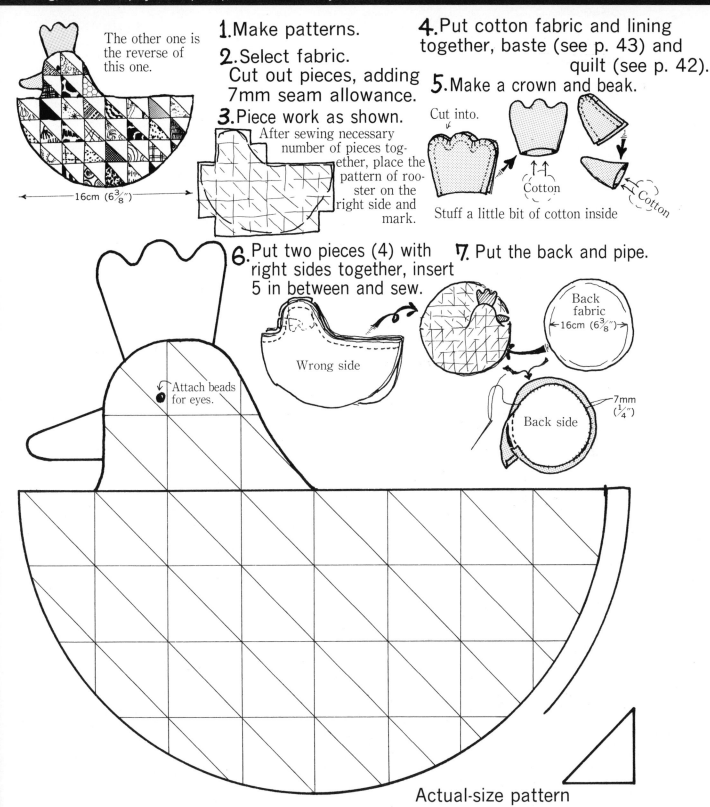

The other one is the reverse of this one.

16cm (6⅜″)

1. Make patterns.

2. Select fabric.
   Cut out pieces, adding 7mm seam allowance.

3. Piece work as shown.
   After sewing necessary number of pieces together, place the pattern of rooster on the right side and mark.

4. Put cotton fabric and lining together, baste (see p. 43) and quilt (see p. 42).

5. Make a crown and beak.
   Cut into.
   Cotton
   Cotton
   Stuff a little bit of cotton inside

6. Put two pieces (4) with right sides together, insert 5 in between and sew.
   Wrong side

7. Put the back and pipe.
   Back fabric
   16cm (6⅜″)
   Back side
   7mm (¼″)

Attach beads for eyes.

Actual-size pattern

63

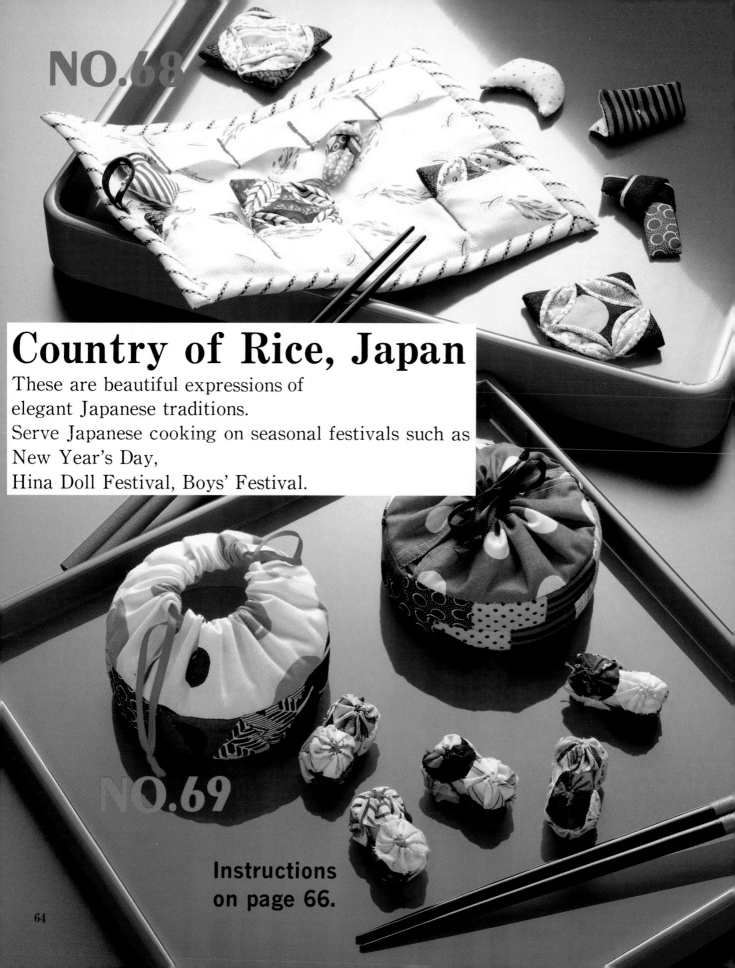

Country of Rice, Japan

These are beautiful expressions of
elegant Japanese traditions.
Serve Japanese cooking on seasonal festivals such as
New Year's Day,
Hina Doll Festival, Boys' Festival.

**Instructions
on page 66.**

Cutlery Case West

Clean silver knives and forks and put them into a little pig's case.
Put a set of cutlery into a mother pig's case. Beal cute and fun!

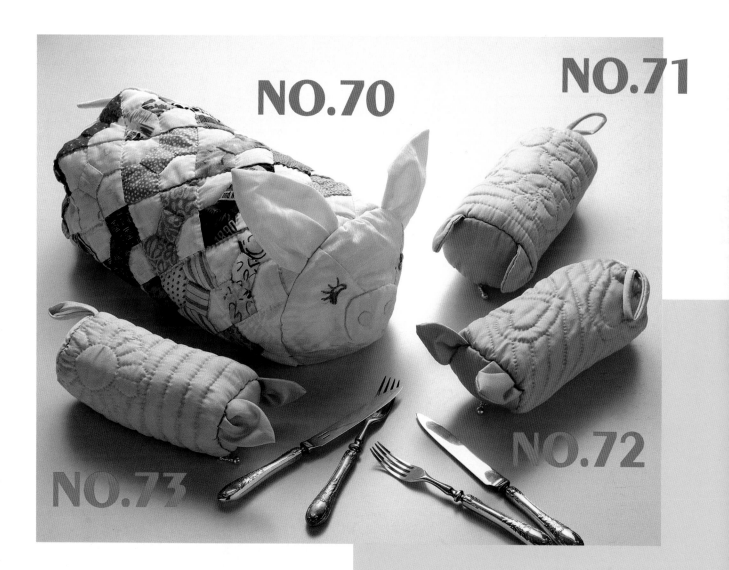

NO.70

NO.71

NO.72

NO.73

Instructions on page 67.

Country of Rice, Japan   p. 64

Materials   No. 68: fabric for patterns, a little; cotton fabric, 30cm(11¾") by 30cm(11¾"); fabric for lining, 25cm(10") by 20cm(7¾"); No. 25 embroidey thread, a little; one button; synthetic cotton, a little;   No 69: fabric for patterns, a little; cotton fabric, fabric for lining, 35cm(13¾") by 20cm(7¾") each; 25cm(10") strings, 4; synthetic cotton, a little.

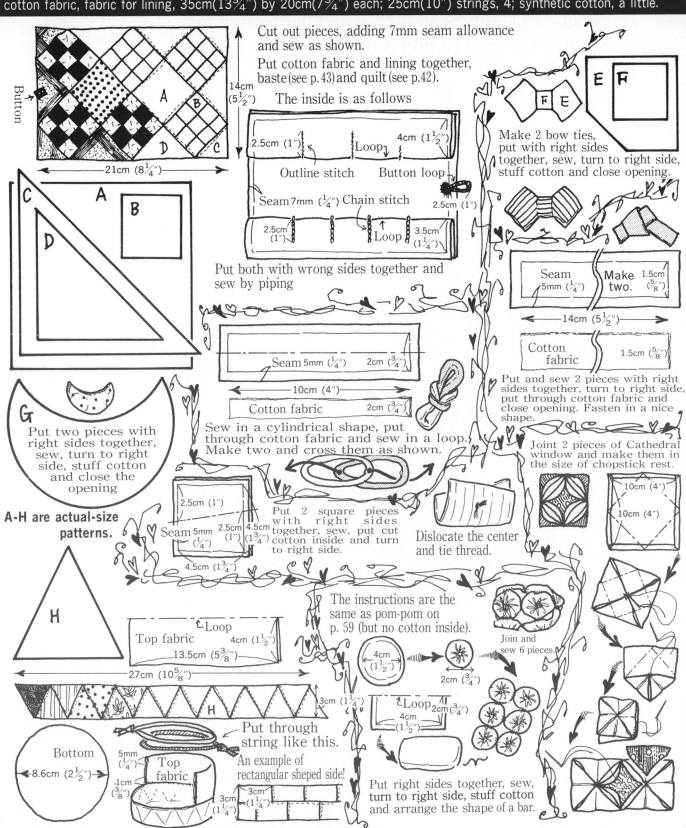

Button

21cm (8¼")

Cut out pieces, adding 7mm seam allowance and sew as shown.

Put cotton fabric and lining together, baste (see p.43) and quilt (see p.42).

The inside is as follows

14cm (5½")

A   B   D   C

C   A   B   D

2.5cm (1")   Loop   4cm (1½")

Outline stitch   Button loop

Seam 7mm (¼") Chain stitch   2.5cm (1")

2.5cm (1")   Loop   3.5cm (1¼")

Put both with wrong sides together and sew by piping

Seam 5mm (¼")   2cm (¾")

10cm (4")

Cotton fabric   2cm (¾")

Sew in a cylindrical shape, put through cotton fabric and sew in a loop. Make two and cross them as shown.

G   Put two pieces with right sides together, sew, turn to right side, stuff cotton and close the opening

A-H are actual-size patterns.

2.5cm (1")

Seam 5mm (¼")   2.5cm (1")   4.5cm (1¾")

4.5cm (1¾")

Put 2 square pieces with right sides together, sew, put cut cotton inside and turn to right side.

Dislocate the center and tie thread.

H

The instructions are the same as pom-pom on p. 59 (but no cotton inside).

E   F   F   E   E   F   F

Make 2 bow ties, put with right sides together, sew, turn to right side, stuff cotton and close opening.

Seam 5mm (¼")   Make two.   1.5cm (⅝")

14cm (5½")

Cotton fabric   1.5cm (⅝")

Put and sew 2 pieces with right sides together, turn to right side, put through cotton fabric and close opening. Fasten in a nice shape.

Joint 2 pieces of Cathedral window and make them in the size of chopstick rest.

10cm (4")   10cm (4")

Loop   Top fabric   4cm (1½")

13.5cm (5⅜")

27cm (10⅝")

H

3cm (1¼")

Put through string like this.

Bottom   8.6cm (2½")

5mm (¼")   Top fabric   .1cm (⅜")   3cm (1¼")

An example of rectangular sheped side!

Loop 2cm (¾")   4cm (1½")

Join and sew 6 pieces.

4cm (1½")   2cm (¾")

3cm (1¼")

Put right sides together, sew, turn to right side, stuff cotton and arrange the shape of a bar.

Cutlery Case-West P. 65

Materials　No. 70: natural color fabric, cotton fabric, fabric for lining, 60cm(23⅝″) square each; fabric for patterns, a little; 30cm(11¾″) zipper; No. 25 embroidery thread, a little; synthetic cotton, a little　Nos. 71 -73: front fabric, cotton fabric, fabric for lining, 40cm(15¾″) by 30cm(11¾″) each; 17cm(6⅝″) zipper

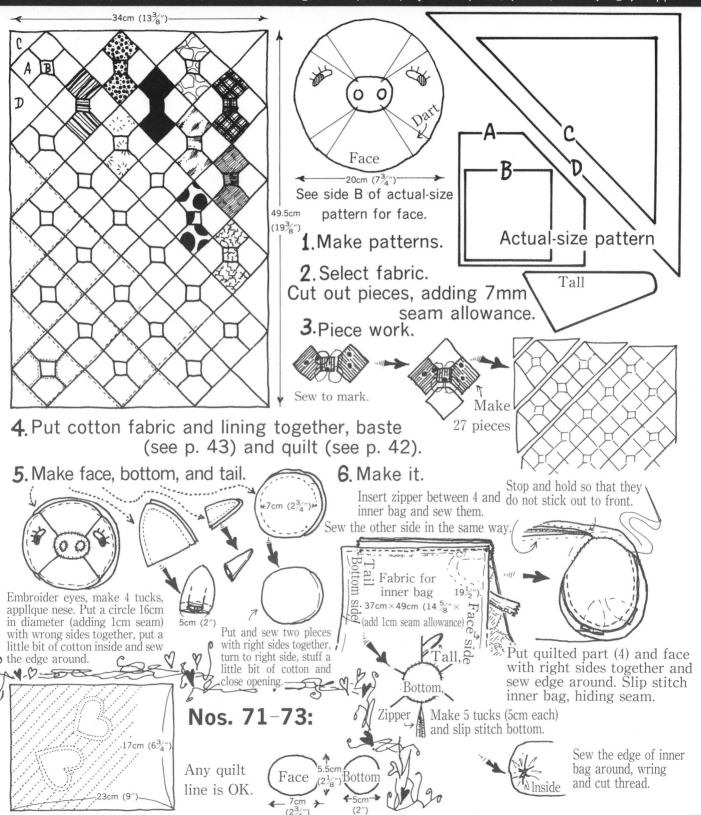

34cm (13⅜″)

49.5cm (19⅜″)

C A B D

Face

20cm (7¾″)

See side B of actual-size pattern for face.

1. Make patterns.

2. Select fabric.
Cut out pieces, adding 7mm seam allowance.

3. Piece work.

Sew to mark.

Make 27 pieces

A C B D

Actual-size pattern

Tall

Dart

4. Put cotton fabric and lining together, baste (see p. 43) and quilt (see p. 42).

5. Make face, bottom, and tail.

7cm (2¾″)

5cm (2″)

Embroider eyes, make 4 tucks, appllque nese. Put a circle 16cm in diameter (adding 1cm seam) with wrong sides together, put a little bit of cotton inside and sew the edge around.

Put and sew two pleces with right sides together, turn to right side, stuff a little bit of cotton and close opening.

17cm (6¾″)

23cm (9″)

Nos. 71-73:

Any quilt line is OK.

Face

Bottom

5.5cm (2⅛″)

7cm (2¾″)

5cm (2″)

6. Make it.

Insert zipper between 4 and inner bag and sew them.
Sew the other side in the same way.

Stop and hold so that they do not stick out to front.

Tall Bottom side

Fabric for inner bag 19½″).
37cm×49cm (14⅝″× (add 1cm seam allowance)

Face side

Tall,

Bottom,

Zipper

Put quilted part (4) and face with right sides together and sew edge around. Slip stitch inner bag, hiding seam.

Make 5 tucks (5cm each) and slip stitch bottom.

Inside

Sew the edge of inner bag around, wring and cut thread.

67

Variation of Hexagon Part II

Colorful items on the dresser
welcome you every morning.
Why don't you start
with this easy patchwork?

NO.74

Instructions on peges 70 and 71.

NO.77

NO.76

NO.77

NO.78

NO.79

NO.80

NO.81

Variation of Hexagon Part II   pp. 68, 69

Materials No.74; fabric for patterns, a little; cotton fabric, fabric for lining, 50cm(19⅝″) by 30cm(11¾″) each; illustration board, 30cm(11¾″) by 25cm(10″); No. 25 embroidery thread, a little; 1.3cm(½″) wide ribbon, 70cm(27⅝″); basket; No. 75 fabric for patterns, a little; cotton fabric, fabric for lining, 50cm(19⅝″) by 15cm(6″) each; No. 76: fabric for patterns, a little; cotton fabric, fabric for lining, 50cm(19⅝″) by 10cm(4″); 25cm(10″) zipper; No. 77: fabric for patterns, a little; cotton fabric, fabric for lining, 40cm(15¾″) by 20cm(7¾″) each; No. 78; fabric for patterns, a little; cotton fabric, fabric for lining, 50cm(19⅝″)

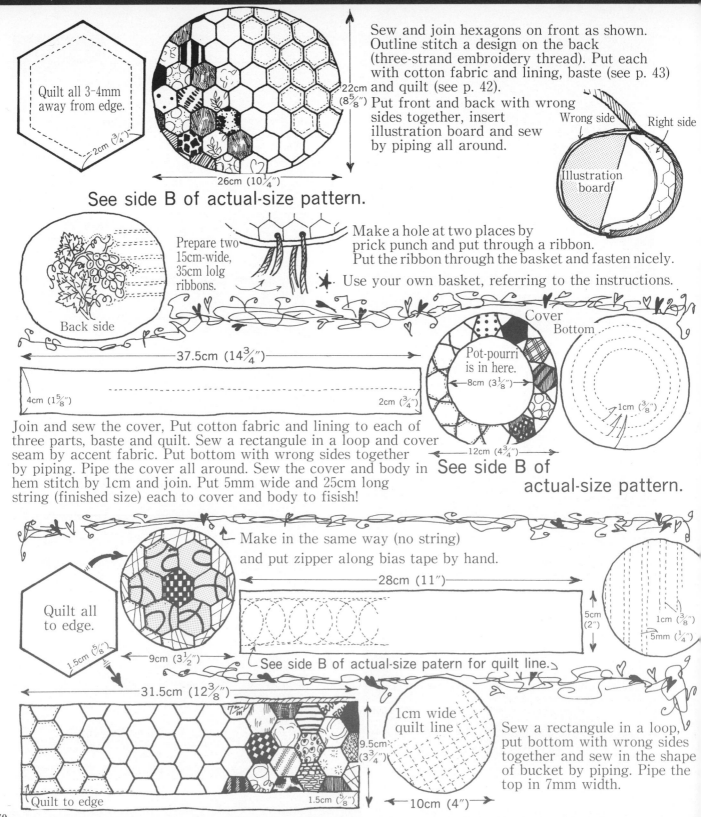

Quilt all 3-4mm away from edge.

2cm (¾″)

22cm (8⅝″)

26cm (10¼″)

See side B of actual-size pattern.

Sew and join hexagons on front as shown. Outline stitch a design on the back (three-strand embroidery thread). Put each with cotton fabric and lining, baste (see p. 43) and quilt (see p. 42). Put front and back with wrong sides together, insert illustration board and sew by piping all around.

Wrong side   Right side

Illustration board

Back side

Prepare two 15cm-wide, 35cm lolg ribbons.

Make a hole at two places by prick punch and put through a ribbon. Put the ribbon through the basket and fasten nicely.

Use your own basket, referring to the instructions.

37.5cm (14¾″)

4cm (1⅝″)   2cm (¾″)

Cover

Bottom

Pot-pourri is in here.

8cm (3⅛″)

1cm (⅜″)

12cm (4¾″)

See side B of actual-size pattern.

Join and sew the cover, Put cotton fabric and lining to each of three parts, baste and quilt. Sew a rectangle in a loop and cover seam by accent fabric. Put bottom with wrong sides together by piping. Pipe the cover all around. Sew the cover and body in hem stitch by 1cm and join. Put 5mm wide and 25cm long string (finished size) each to cover and body to fisish!

Make in the same way (no string) and put zipper along bias tape by hand.

Quilt all to edge.

1.5cm (⅝″)

9cm (3½″)

28cm (11″)

5cm (2″)

1cm (⅜″)

5mm (¼″)

See side B of actual-size patern for quilt line.

31.5cm (12⅜″)

1cm wide quilt line

9.5cm (3¾″)

Quilt to edge

1.5cm (⅝″)

10cm (4″)

Sew a rectangle in a loop, put bottom with wrong sides together and sew in the shape of bucket by piping. Pipe the top in 7mm width.

square each; No. 79; fabric for patterns, a little; cotton fabric, fabric for lining, 50cm(19⅝″) by 40cm(15¾″) each; synthetic cotton; string; proper quantity; No. 80: fabric for patterns, a little; cotton fabric, fabric for lining, 40cm(15¾″) square each; 6mm(¼″)-wide flat elastic, 11cm(4⅜″); No. 81 fabric for patterns, a little; cotton fabric, fabric for lining, 50cm(19⅝″) by 25cm(10″) each

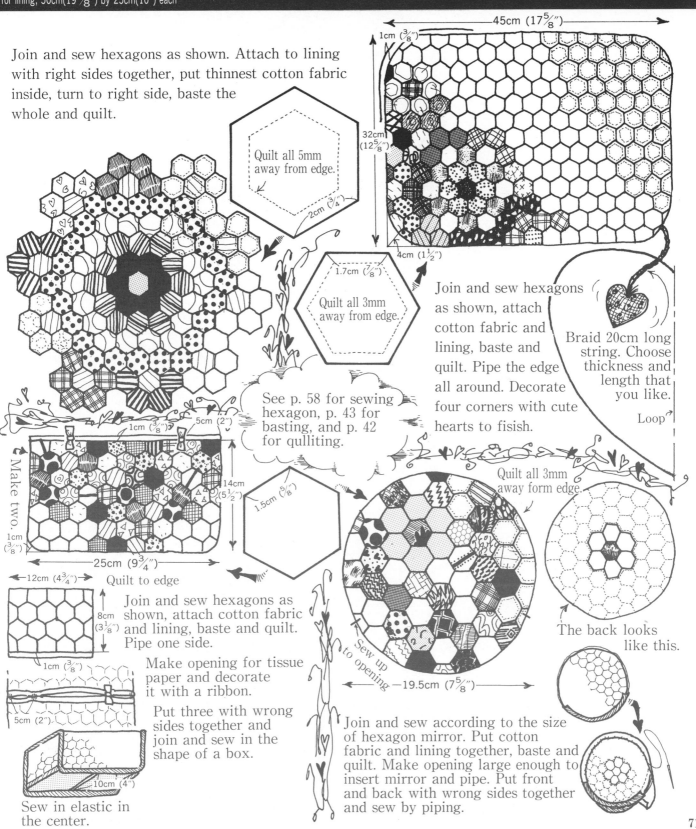

Join and sew hexagons as shown. Attach to lining with right sides together, put thinnest cotton fabric inside, turn to right side, baste the whole and quilt.

45cm (17⅝″)

1cm (3/8″)

32cm (12⅝″)

4cm (1½″)

Quilt all 5mm away from edge.

2cm (¾″)

1.7cm (7/8″)

Quilt all 3mm away from edge.

Join and sew hexagons as shown, attach cotton fabric and lining, baste and quilt. Pipe the edge all around. Decorate four corners with cute hearts to fisish.

Braid 20cm long string. Choose thickness and length that you like.

Loop

See p. 58 for sewing hexagon, p. 43 for basting, and p. 42 for qulliting.

Make two.

1cm (3/8″)

5cm (2″)

14cm (5½″)

1cm (3/8″)

25cm (9¾″)

1.5cm (5/8″)

Quilt all 3mm away form edge.

12cm (4¾″)

Quilt to edge

8cm (3⅛″)

Join and sew hexagons as shown, attach cotton fabric and lining, baste and quilt. Pipe one side.

Make opening for tissue paper and decorate it with a ribbon.

Put three with wrong sides together and join and sew in the shape of a box.

1cm (3/8″)

5cm (2″)

10cm (4″)

Sew in elastic in the center.

Sew up to opening

19.5cm (7⅝″)

The back looks like this.

Join and sew according to the size of hexagon mirror. Put cotton fabric and lining together, baste and quilt. Make opening large enough to insert mirror and pipe. Put front and back with wrong sides together and sew by piping.

71

NO.82

NO.83

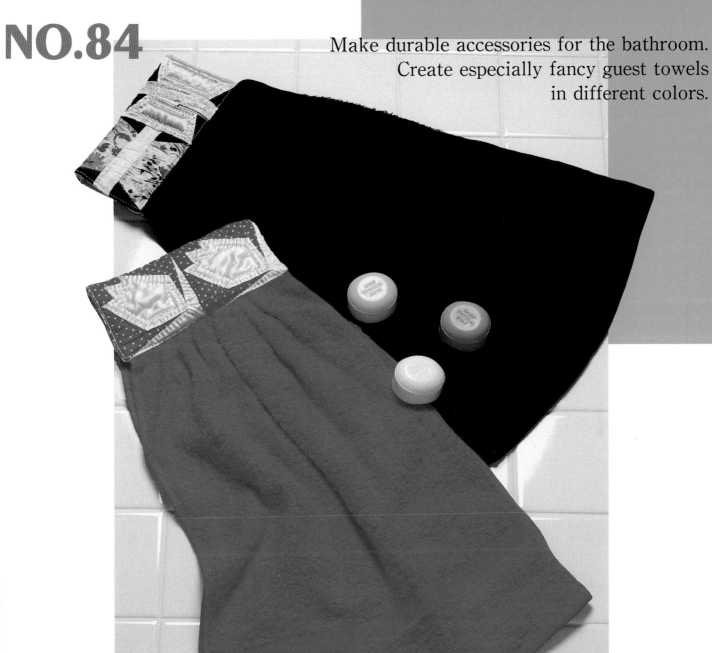

Clean and Comfortable Bathroom

Make durable accessories for the bathroom.
Create especially fancy guest towels
in different colors.

Instructions on pages 74 and 75.

Clean and Comfortable toilet p.p. 72, 73

Materials No. 83 (top cover): fabric for patterns, a little; cotton fabric, fabric for lining, 55cm(21⅝″) by 55cm(21⅝″) each; 1.5cm(⅝″)-wide flat elastic, 25cm(10″); 1cm(⅜″)-wide flat elastic, 80cm(31⅜″)
No. 83 (mat): fabric for patterns, a little; cotton fabric, fabric for lining; 70cm(27⅝″) each;

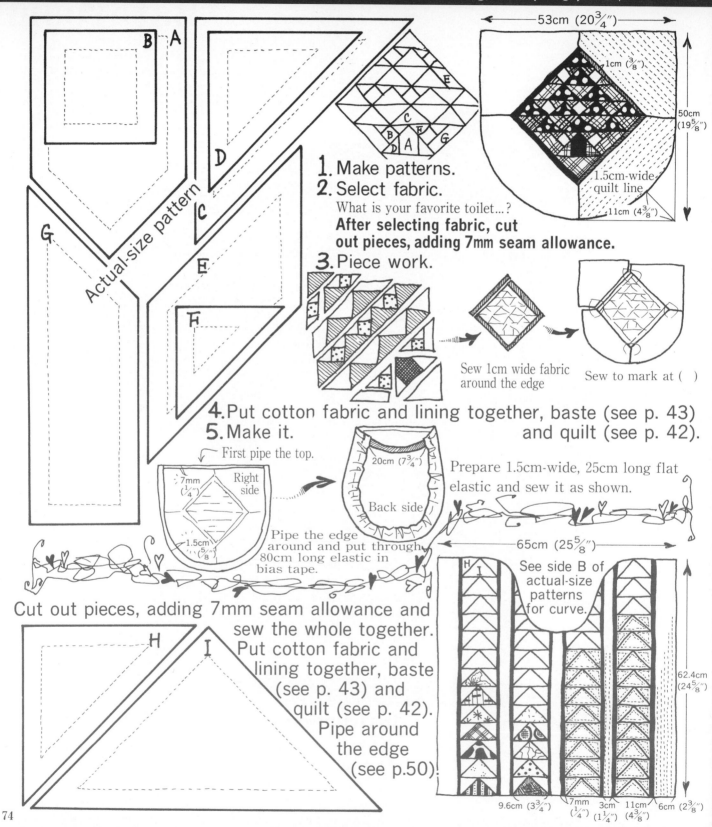

Actual-size pattern

53cm (20¾″)

50cm (19⅝″)

1cm (⅜″)

1.5cm-wide quilt line

11cm (4⅜″)

1. Make patterns.
2. Select fabric.
What is your favorite toilet...?
After selecting fabric, cut out pieces, adding 7mm seam allowance.
3. Piece work.

Sew 1cm wide fabric around the edge

Sew to mark at ( )

4. Put cotton fabric and lining together, baste (see p. 43) and quilt (see p. 42).
5. Make it.

First pipe the top.

7mm (¼″)   Right side

1.5cm (⅝″)

20cm (7¾″)

Back side

Pipe the edge around and put through 80cm long elastic in bias tape.

Prepare 1.5cm-wide, 25cm long flat elastic and sew it as shown.

65cm (25⅝″)

See side B of actual-size patterns for curve.

62.4cm (24⅝″)

Cut out pieces, adding 7mm seam allowance and sew the whole together. Put cotton fabric and lining together, baste (see p. 43) and quilt (see p. 42). Pipe around the edge (see p.50).

9.6cm (3¾″)   7mm (¼″)   3cm (1¼″)   11cm (4⅜″)   6cm (2⅜″)

74

No. 82; fabric for patterns, a little; cotton fabric, fabric for lining, 75cm(29⅝″) by 20cm(7¾″) each;
Nos. 84, 85: fabric for patterns, a little; cotton fabric, fabric for lining, fabric for back, 20cm(7¾″) by 20cm(7¾″) each; 1 towel; magic tape

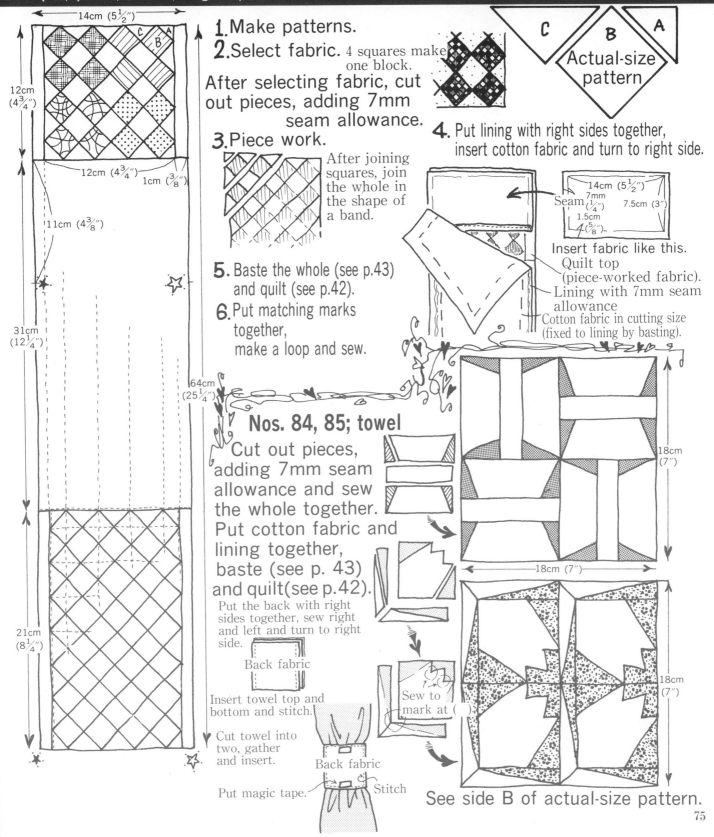

1. Make patterns.
2. Select fabric. 4 squares make one block.
After selecting fabric, cut out pieces, adding 7mm seam allowance.
3. Piece work.

After joining squares, join the whole in the shape of a band.

Actual-size pattern

4. Put lining with right sides together, insert cotton fabric and turn to right side.

Seam
14cm (5½″)
7mm (¼″)
7.5cm (3″)
1.5cm (⅝″)

Insert fabric like this.
Quilt top (piece-worked fabric).
Lining with 7mm seam allowance
Cotton fabric in cutting size (fixed to lining by basting).

5. Baste the whole (see p.43) and quilt (see p.42).
6. Put matching marks together, make a loop and sew.

Nos. 84, 85; towel

Cut out pieces, adding 7mm seam allowance and sew the whole together. Put cotton fabric and lining together, baste (see p. 43) and quilt(see p.42).

Put the back with right sides together, sew right and left and turn to right side.

Back fabric

Insert towel top and bottom and stitch.

Cut towel into two, gather and insert.

Back fabric

Put magic tape.

Stitch

Sew to mark at ( )

See side B of actual-size pattern.

14cm (5½″)
12cm (4¾″)
12cm (4¾″)
1cm (⅜″)
11cm (4⅜″)
31cm (12¼″)
64cm (25¼″)
21cm (8¼″)
18cm (7″)
18cm (7″)
18cm (7″)

Cosmetic Case/5 types

Put cosmetics in the bag.
Their patterns are like
miniature baskets.
Which is your favorite
among the five?

**Instructions
on page 78.**

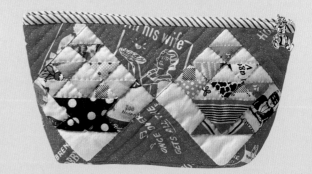

Bostonbag-type petit bags/5 types

These cute designs can be used both by small kids and adults. Enjoy them as you like.

NO.91

NO.92

Instructions on page 79.

NO.93

NO.95

NO.94

Materials

Nos. 86-90: fabric for patterns, a little; cotton fabric, fabric for lining, 30cm(11¾″) by 30cm(11¾″) each; 20cm(7¾″) zipper

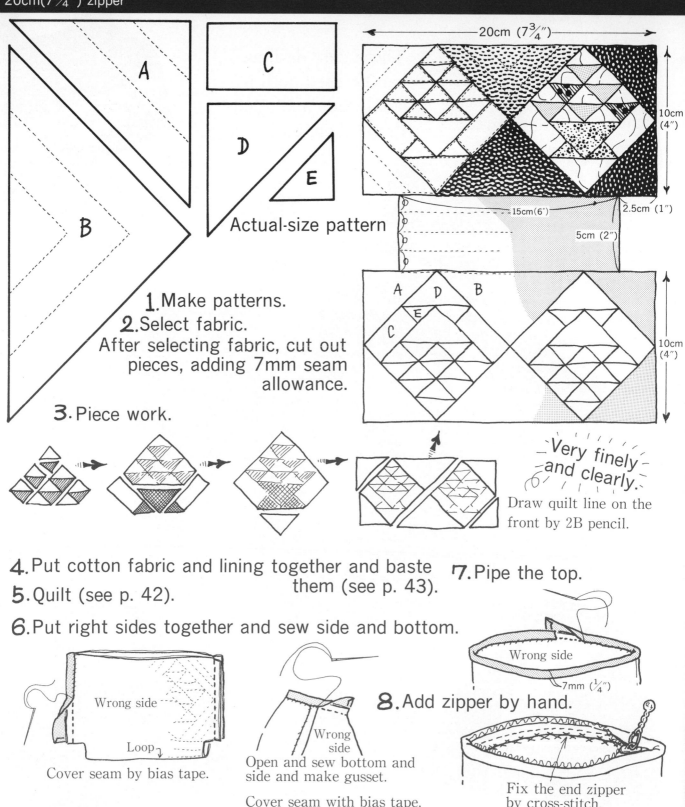

A
C
D
E
B

Actual-size pattern

20cm (7¾″)

10cm (4″)

15cm(6″)

2.5cm (1″)

5cm (2″)

A   D   B
C   E

10cm (4″)

1. Make patterns.
2. Select fabric.
After selecting fabric, cut out pieces, adding 7mm seam allowance.
3. Piece work.

Very finely and clearly.

Draw quilt line on the front by 2B pencil.

4. Put cotton fabric and lining together and baste them (see p. 43).
5. Quilt (see p. 42).
6. Put right sides together and sew side and bottom.
7. Pipe the top.

Wrong side

Loop

Cover seam by bias tape.

Wrong side

Open and sew bottom and side and make gusset.

Cover seam with bias tape.

Wrong side

7mm (¼″)

8. Add zipper by hand.

Fix the end zipper by cross-stitch.

Bostonbag-type petit bags/5 types   p.77

Materials

Nos. 91-95: fabric for patterns, a little; cotton fabric, fabric for lining, 45cm(17⅝″) by 35cm(13¾″) each;
30cm(11¾″) zipper

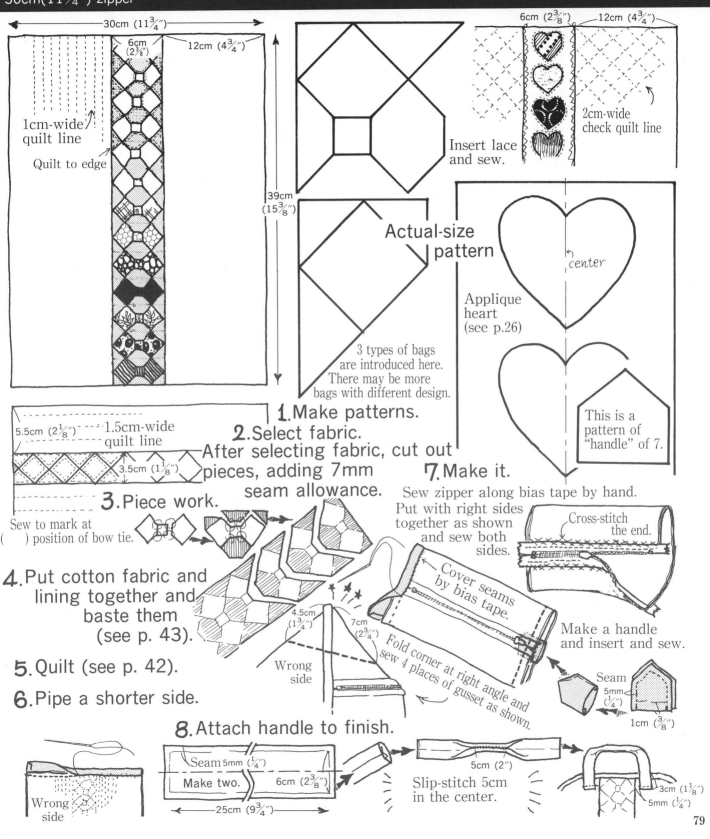

30cm (11¾″)

6cm (2⅜″)   12cm (4¾″)

1cm-wide quilt line

Quilt to edge

39cm (15⅜″)

6cm (2⅜″)   12cm (4¾″)

Insert lace and sew.

2cm-wide check quilt line

Actual-size pattern

center

Applique heart (see p.26)

3 types of bags are introduced here. There may be more bags with different design.

This is a pattern of "handle" of 7.

5.5cm (2⅛″)   1.5cm-wide quilt line

3.5cm (1⅛″)

Sew to mark at ( ) position of bow tie.

1. Make patterns.

2. Select fabric.
After selecting fabric, cut out pieces, adding 7mm seam allowance.

3. Piece work.

7. Make it.
Sew zipper along bias tape by hand. Put with right sides together as shown and sew both sides.

Cross-stitch the end.

Cover seams by bias tape.

Make a handle and insert and sew.

4. Put cotton fabric and lining together and baste them (see p. 43).

5. Quilt (see p. 42).

6. Pipe a shorter side.

4.5cm (1¾″)

7cm (2¾″)

Wrong side

Fold corner at right angle and sew 4 places of gusset as shown.

Seam 5mm (¼″)

1cm (⅜″)

8. Attach handle to finish.

Wrong side

Seam 5mm (¼″)

Make two.   6cm (2⅜″)

25cm (9¾″)

5cm (2″)

Slip-stitch 5cm in the center.

3cm (1⅛″)

5mm (¼″)

79

Large
shopping bags/4 types

A basket-type wheat bag and bags
with pinwheel patterns.
How about doing your shopping with
a handmade bag ? It's elegant and helps
the environment.

NO.96

NO.97

Instructions
on pages 82 and 83.

NO.98

NO.99

Materials No. 96: white, 70cm(27⅝″) by 70cm(27⅝″) fabric for patterns of basket, 1m(39⅜″) by 40cm(15¾″); cotton fabric, fabric for lining, 1m(39⅜″) by 80cm(31⅜″); inner bag, 85cm(33⅜″) by 85cm(33⅜″); No.25 embroidery thread, a little; 2.5cm(1″)-wide cotton tape, 1m30cm(51⅛″); 50cm(19⅝″) zipper;   metal fitting, 4

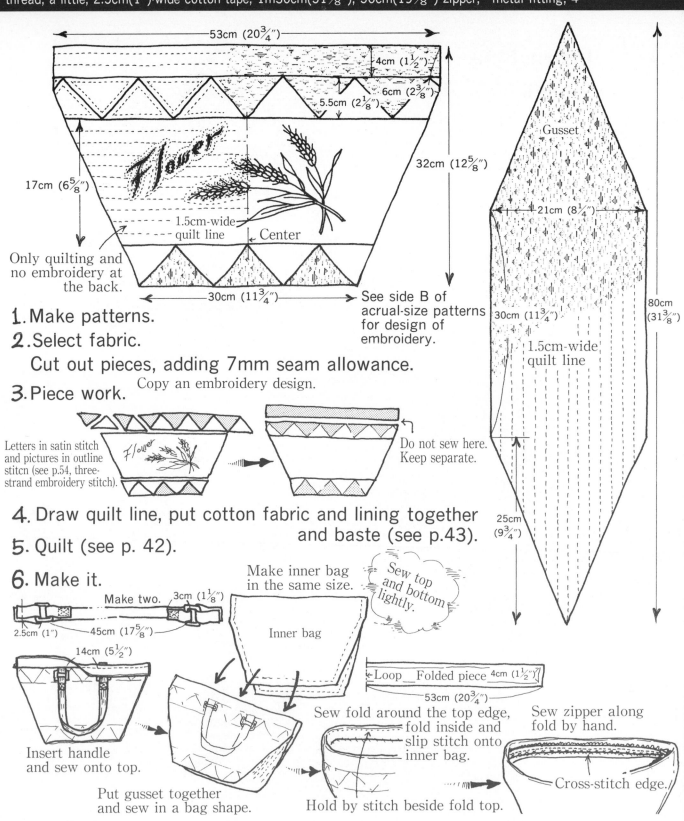

53cm (20¾″)

4cm (1½″)

6cm (2⅜″)

5.5cm (2⅛″)

32cm (12⅝″)

17cm (6⅝″)

Flower

1.5cm-wide quilt line

Center

Only quilting and no embroidery at the back.

30cm (11¾″)

See side B of acrual-size patterns for design of embroidery.

Gusset

21cm (8¼″)

80cm (31⅜″)

30cm (11¾″)

1.5cm-wide quilt line

25cm (9¾″)

1. Make patterns.
2. Select fabric.
Cut out pieces, adding 7mm seam allowance.
3. Piece work.
Copy an embroidery design.

Letters in satin stitch and pictures in outline stitcn (see p.54, three-strand embroidery stitch).

Flower

Do not sew here. Keep separate.

4. Draw quilt line, put cotton fabric and lining together and baste (see p.43).
5. Quilt (see p. 42).
6. Make it.

Make two. 3cm (1⅛″)

2.5cm (1″)   45cm (17⅝″)

14cm (5½″)

Make inner bag in the same size.

Inner bag

Sew top and bottom lightly.

Loop Folded piece 4cm (1½″)

53cm (20¾″)

Insert handle and sew onto top.

Put gusset together and sew in a bag shape.

Sew fold around the top edge, fold inside and slip stitch onto inner bag.

Hold by stitch beside fold top.

Sew zipper along fold by hand.

Cross-stitch edge.

Nos. 97-99: fabric for patterns, a little; cotton fabric, fabric for lining, 80cm(31⅜″) by 40cm(15¾″) each; fabric for back, 80cm(31⅜″) by 65cm(25⅝″); core, 60cm(23⅝″) by 10cm(4″)

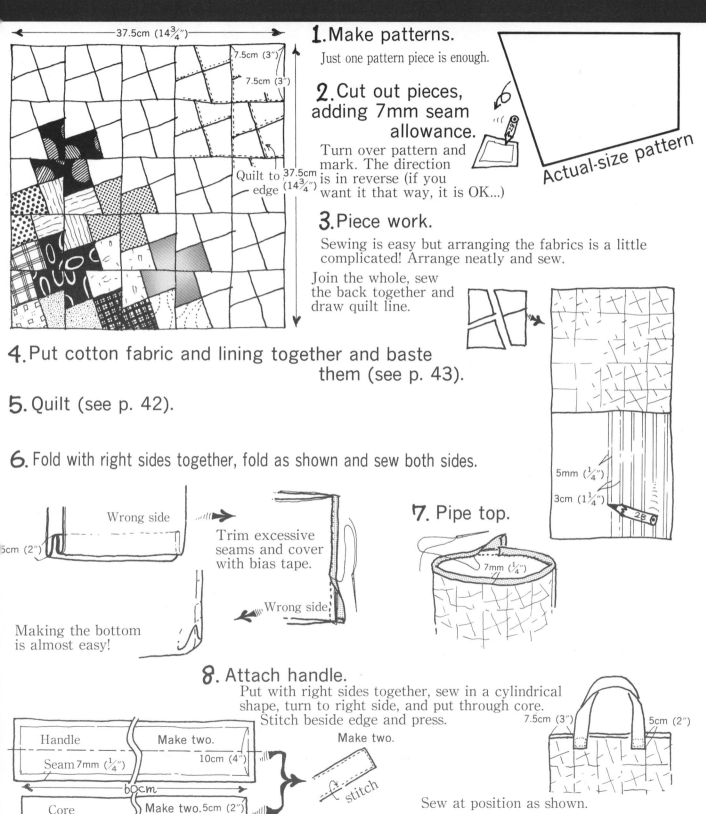

37.5cm (14¾″)

7.5cm (3″)

7.5cm (3″)

Quilt to edge

37.5cm (14¾″)

1. Make patterns.

Just one pattern piece is enough.

2. Cut out pieces, adding 7mm seam allowance.

Turn over pattern and mark. The direction is in reverse (if you want it that way, it is OK...)

Actual-size pattern

3. Piece work.

Sewing is easy but arranging the fabrics is a little complicated! Arrange neatly and sew.

Join the whole, sew the back together and draw quilt line.

4. Put cotton fabric and lining together and baste them (see p. 43).

(see p. 43)

5. Quilt (see p. 42).

(see p. 42)

6. Fold with right sides together, fold as shown and sew both sides.

Wrong side

5cm (2″)

Trim excessive seams and cover with bias tape.

Wrong side

Making the bottom is almost easy!

7. Pipe top.

7mm (¼″)

5mm (¼″)

3cm (1¼″)

28

8. Attach handle.

Put with right sides together, sew in a cylindrical shape, turn to right side, and put through core. Stitch beside edge and press.

Make two.

Handle

Seam 7mm (¼″)

Make two.

10cm (4″)

60cm

Core

Make two. 5cm (2″)

stitch

7.5cm (3″)

5cm (2″)

Sew at position as shown.

NO.100

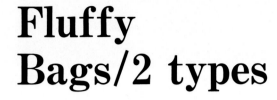

Fluffy Bags/2 types

These dice-shaped small bags look trendy, don't they ?

NO.103

**Instructions
on pages 86 and 87.**

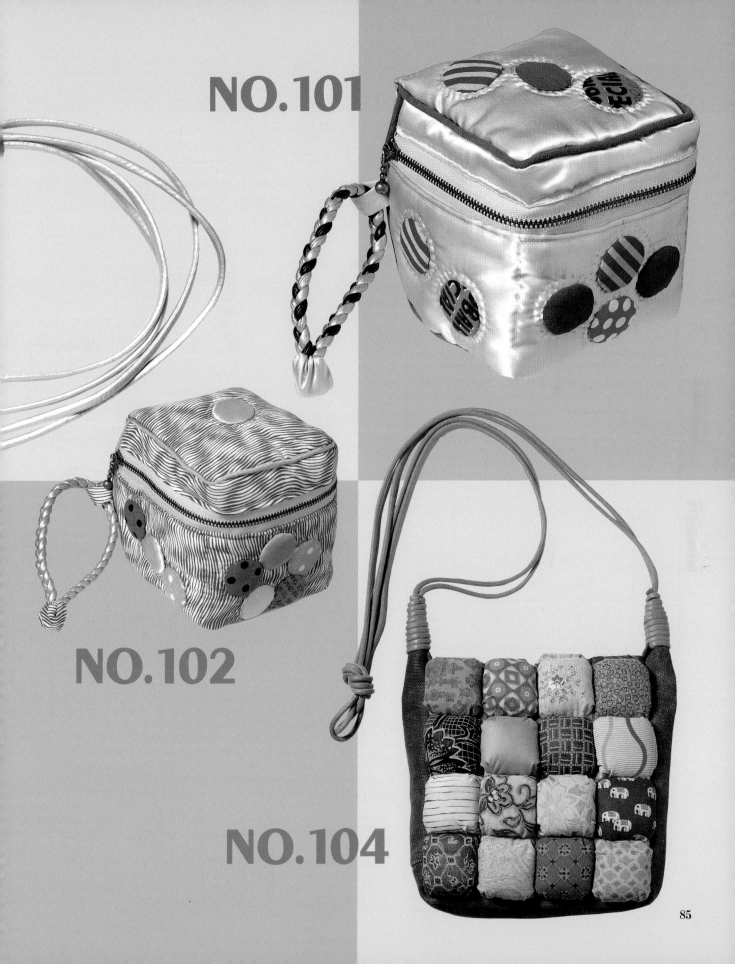

NO.101

NO.102

NO.104

85

Fluffy Bags/2 types PP. 84, 85

Materials

Nos. 103,104: fabric for patterns, a little; case fabric, 60cm(23⅝″) by 30cm(11¾″), fabric for gusset, 60cm(23⅝″) by 20cm(7¾″); inner bag, 50cm(19⅝″) by 25cm(10″); string,7m(275⅝″).

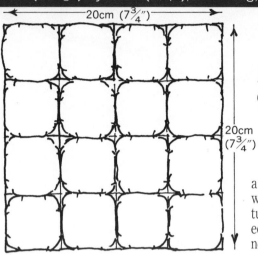

20cm (7¾″)

20cm (7¾″)

1. Make patterns.

2. Select fabric.

After selecting fabric, cut out pieces, adding 7mm seam allowance.

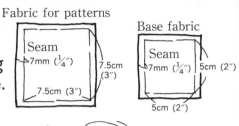

Fabric for patterns

Seam 7mm (¼″)   7.5cm (3″)

7.5cm (3″)

Base fabric

Seam 7mm (¼″)   5cm (2″)

5cm (2″)

3. Make puff.

a. Put base and fabric for patterns with right sides together, make tucks for loose part and sew the edge around (no opening is necessary).

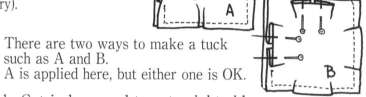

A

B

There are two ways to make a tuck such as A and B.
A is applied here, but either one is OK.

b. Cut in base and turn to right side from here.

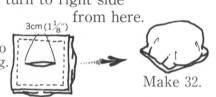

3cm (1⅛″)

Cut along texture to keep from loosening.

Make 32.

Actual-size pattern

Base fabric

Fabric for patterns

c. Put right sides together and slip stitch. Make a stitch beside fabrics for patterns. Put through needle at right angle for neat finish.

90°

Cotton

Use as fine a stitch as possible !

d. Stuff cotton and slip-stitch top. Stuff cotton as you like, but stuff in the same quantity to each puff.

Make two.

4. Make gusset.

Seam 5mm (¼″)   Make two.   6cm (2⅜″)

60cm (23⅝″)

Put two pieces with right sides together, sew, turn to right side and stitch.

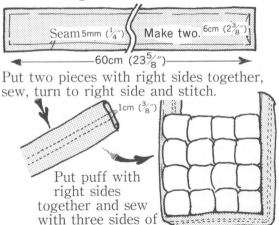

1cm (⅜″)

Put puff with right sides together and sew with three sides of edge in slip stitch.

5. Sew inner bag.

Fold seam and slip stitch gusset and puffs beside edge.

20cm (7¾″)

Fabric for inner bag   20cm (7¾″)

Seam 7mm (¼″)   Make two.

6. Sew string.

Cover tip of handle with fabric for gusset and sew.

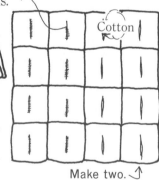

150cm (59″)

Make two.

50cm (19⅝″)

Roll carafuly by a string.

Fasten tip

Nos. 100-102: fabric for patterns, a little; front, cotton fabric, fabric for lining, 40cm(15¾″) by 30cm(11¾″) each; 30cm(11¾″) zipper, 30cm(11¾″) string, 3; yarn, a little

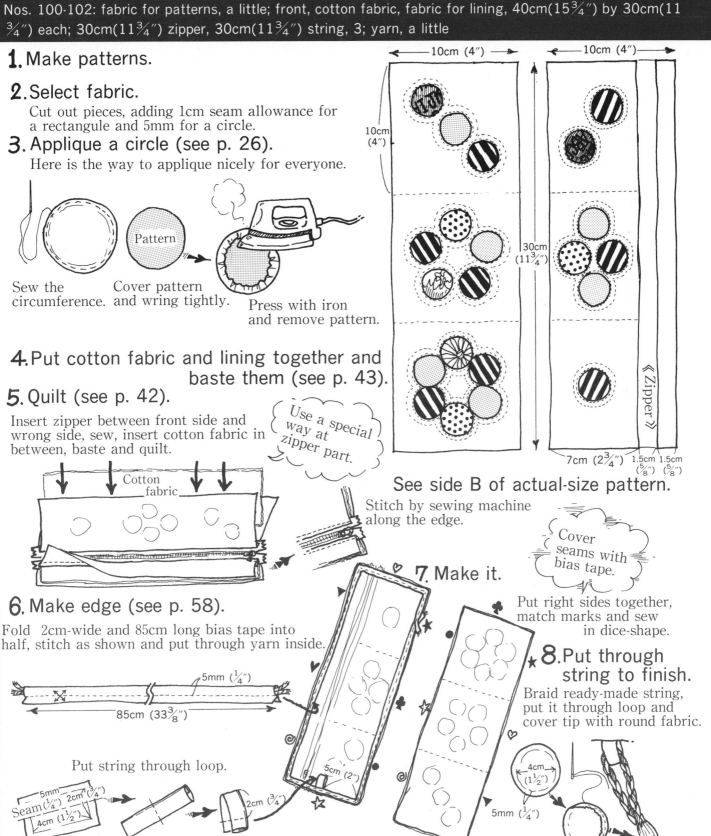

1. Make patterns.

2. Select fabric.

Cut out pieces, adding 1cm seam allowance for a rectangule and 5mm for a circle.

3. Applique a circle (see p. 26).

Here is the way to applique nicely for everyone.

Sew the circumference.

Cover pattern and wring tightly.

Press with iron and remove pattern.

4. Put cotton fabric and lining together and baste them (see p. 43).

5. Quilt (see p. 42).

Insert zipper between front side and wrong side, sew, insert cotton fabric in between, baste and quilt.

Use a special way at zipper part.

Cotton fabric

10cm (4″)   10cm (4″)

10cm (4″)

30cm (11¾″)

《Zipper》

7cm (2¾″)   1.5cm (⅝″) 1.5cm (⅝″)

See side B of actual-size pattern.

Stitch by sewing machine along the edge.

Cover seams with bias tape.

6. Make edge (see p. 58).

Fold 2cm-wide and 85cm long bias tape into half, stitch as shown and put through yarn inside.

5mm (¼″)

85cm (33⅜″)

7. Make it.

Put right sides together, match marks and sew in dice-shape.

8. Put through string to finish.

Braid ready-made string, put it through loop and cover tip with round fabric.

Put string through loop.

Seam (¼″)   2cm (¾″)   2cm (¾″)
4cm (1½″)

2cm (¾″)

5cm (2″)

4cm (1½″)

5mm (¼″)

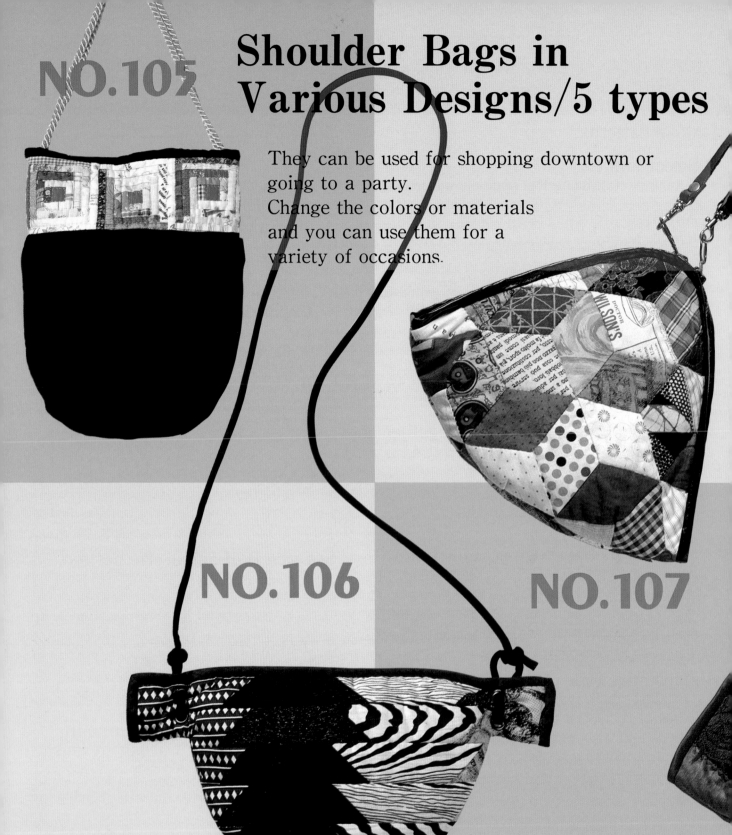

Shoulder Bags in Various Designs/5 types

They can be used for shopping downtown or going to a party.
Change the colors or materials and you can use them for a variety of occasions.

NO.105

NO.106

NO.107

**Instructions
on pages 90 and 91.**

NO.109

NO.108

Materials   No. 107: fabric for patterns, a little; cotton fabric, fabric for lining, 60cm(23⅝″) by 35cm(13¾″) each; 21cm(8¼″) zipper 2; leather tape, 1m(39⅜″); leather string, 1m20cm(47⅛″); loop clutch, 2   Nos. 108: black, a little; cotton fabric and fabric for lining, 60cm(23⅝″) by 35cm(13¾″) each; 21cm(8¼″) zipper, 2; leather tape, 1m(39⅜″); leather string, 1m20cm(47⅛″); loop clutch, 2

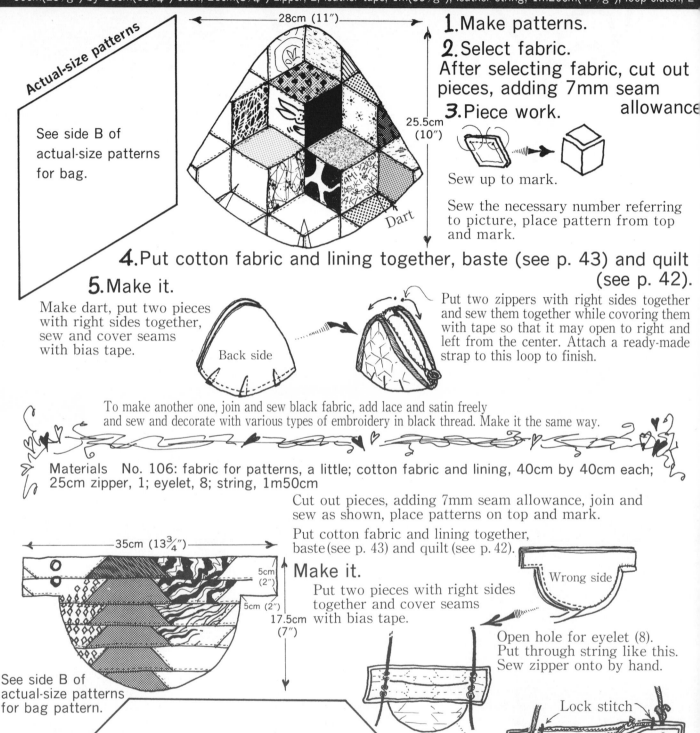

Actual-size patterns

28cm (11″)

See side B of actual-size patterns for bag.

25.5cm (10″)

Dart

1. Make patterns.

2. Select fabric.
After selecting fabric, cut out pieces, adding 7mm seam allowance

3. Piece work.

Sew up to mark.

Sew the necessary number referring to picture, place pattern from top and mark.

4. Put cotton fabric and lining together, baste (see p. 43) and quilt (see p. 42).

5. Make it.

Make dart, put two pieces with right sides together, sew and cover seams with bias tape.

Back side

Put two zippers with right sides together and sew them together while covoring them with tape so that it may open to right and left from the center. Attach a ready-made strap to this loop to finish.

To make another one, join and sew black fabric, add lace and satin freely and sew and decorate with various types of embroidery in black thread. Make it the same way.

Materials   No. 106: fabric for patterns, a little; cotton fabric and lining, 40cm by 40cm each; 25cm zipper, 1; eyelet, 8; string, 1m50cm

Cut out pieces, adding 7mm seam allowance, join and sew as shown, place patterns on top and mark.

Put cotton fabric and lining together, baste (see p. 43) and quilt (see p. 42).

Make it.

Put two pieces with right sides together and cover seams with bias tape.

35cm (13¾″)

5cm (2″)

5cm (2″)

17.5cm (7″)

See side B of actual-size patterns for bag pattern.

Actual-size pattern

Wrong side

Open hole for eyelet (8). Put through string like this. Sew zipper onto by hand.

Lock stitch

No. 109: yellow, 1m30cm(51⅜″) by 50cm(19⅝″); fabric for patterns, a little; cotton fabric, fabric for lining, 70cm(27⅝″) by 60cm(23⅝″) each; a set of metal fittings; core, 2.5cm(1″) by 1m30cm(51⅜″); magic tape.

No. 105: fabric for patterns, a little; cotton fabric and fabric for lining, 55cm(21⅝″) by 10cm(4½″) each; black velvet, fabric for inner lining, 50cm(19⅝″) by 30cm(11¾″) each; string, 1m70cm(66¾″)

B. Bag body

16cm (6⅜″)

25cm (9¾″)

C. Front pocket

14cm (5½″)

25cm (9¾″)

See side B of actual-size pattern.

A. Bag body

30cm (11¾″)

25cm (9¾″)

50cm (19⅝″)

F. Pocket gusset 3cm

53cm (20¾″)

E. Body gusset. 5cm

D. Back pocket.

14.5cm (5¾″)

25cm (9¾″)

Cut out pieces for each part from A through F, join and sew.
Put cotton fabric and lining together,
baste (see p. 43) and quilt (see p. 42).

☆ Make a bag.

1. Put C and F with right sides together, pipe seams and top.

C. Front

2. Put E and B with right sides together, insert 1 and sew.
Pipe seams and top.

B
C F E

A
D

3. Pipe top of D, place it on A and baste the edge around.

4. Put 2 and 3 with wrong sides together and join and sew by piping.

5. Put magic tape to close cover.

6. Attach handle.

No. 105 Bag

Sew 6 patterns of log cabin, quilt, and sew in a loop.

Put two black fabrics with right sides together, sew with patterns. Pipe by 7mm top.

Make inner bag in the same size as black fabric and slip stitch beside patterns.

Sew string inside.

See side B of actual-size patterns for the pattern of log cabin.

24cm (9⅜″)

8cm (3⅛″)

20cm (7¾″)

5cm (2″)

Seam 5mm (¼″) 5cm (2″)

130cm (53″)

Core

Make string, put through core and stitch (see p. 54).

Sew one side by stitching.

Put metal fittings on the other side to adjust length.

5cm (2″)

5cm (2″)

3cm (1¼″)

2.5cm (1″)

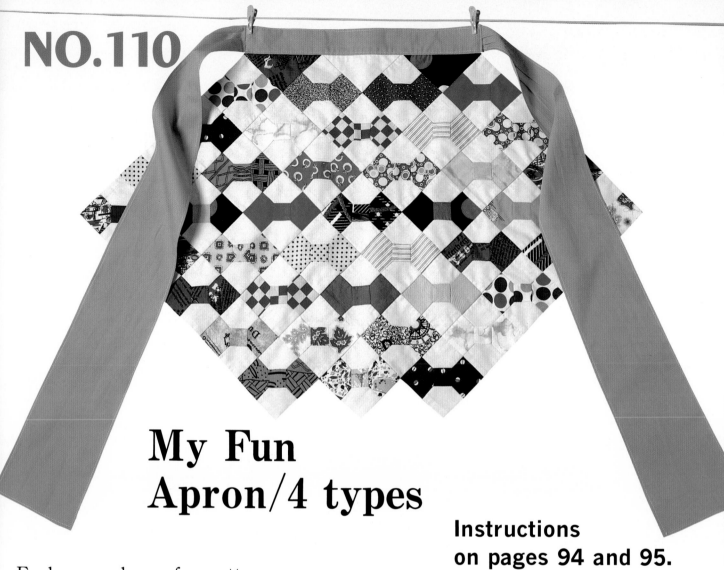

NO.110

My Fun
Apron/4 types

**Instructions
on pages 94 and 95.**

Each apron has a fun pattern.
The pocket of the apron on the hanger can be removed.
They all look so nice.

NO.111

NO.112

NO.113

My fun apron/4 types pp. 92, 93

Materials

No. 110: fabric for patterns, a little; fabric for lining, 50cm(19⅝″) by 40cm(15¾″), string, 1m(39⅜″) by 40cm(15¾″)

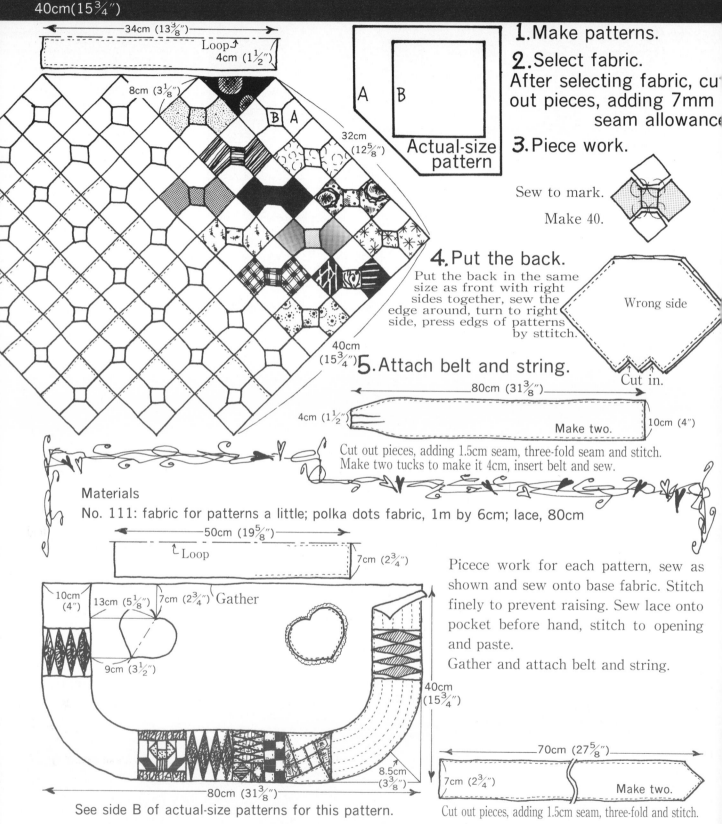

34cm (13⅜″)

Loop↵
4cm (1½″)

8cm (3⅛″)

B A

32cm (12⅝″)

A B

Actual-size pattern

40cm (15¾″)

1. **Make patterns.**

2. **Select fabric.**
After selecting fabric, cut out pieces, adding 7mm seam allowance

3. **Piece work.**

Sew to mark.

Make 40.

4. **Put the back.**
Put the back in the same size as front with right sides together, sew the edge around, turn to right side, press edgs of patterns by sttitch.

5. **Attach belt and string.**

Wrong side

Cut in.

80cm (31⅜″)

4cm (1½″)

Make two.

10cm (4″)

Cut out pieces, adding 1.5cm seam, three-fold seam and stitch. Make two tucks to make it 4cm, insert belt and sew.

Materials

No. 111: fabric for patterns a little; polka dots fabric, 1m by 6cm; lace, 80cm

50cm (19⅝″)

↥ Loop

7cm (2¾″)

10cm (4″)

13cm (5⅛″)

7cm (2¾″) Gather

9cm (3½″)

40cm (15¾″)

8.5cm (3⅜″)

80cm (31⅜″)

See side B of actual-size patterns for this pattern.

Piecece work for each pattern, sew as shown and sew onto base fabric. Stitch finely to prevent raising. Sew lace onto pocket before hand, stitch to opening and paste.

Gather and attach belt and string.

70cm (27⅝″)

7cm (2¾″)

Make two.

Cut out pieces, adding 1.5cm seam, three-fold and stitch.

No. 113: striped fabric, 1m50cm(59″) by 1m30cm(51⅜″); fabric for patterns, a little; cotton fabric, fabric for lining, 50cm(19⅝″) by 30cm(11¾″) each; 4 buttons, round elastic, 30cm(11¾″);
No, 112: striped fabric, 1m(39⅜″) by 75cm(29⅝″); fabric for patterns, a little

1. Make patterns.
2. Make apron.

Put and sew heart-shaped chest part and heart- shape of shoulder strip together. Sew wrong side in the same size of front side (the same fabric with front is OK). Since chest part and shoulder string are doubled, put two right sides and wrong sides with right sides together, sew, turn to right side and stitch two on edge. Cut out pieces, adding 1.5cm seam allowance for skirt, three-fold edge and stitch. Put buttons on pocket position and gather the upper part. Cross shoulder strings, put and asterisk and belt asterisk together, insert string and skirt into belt and sew.

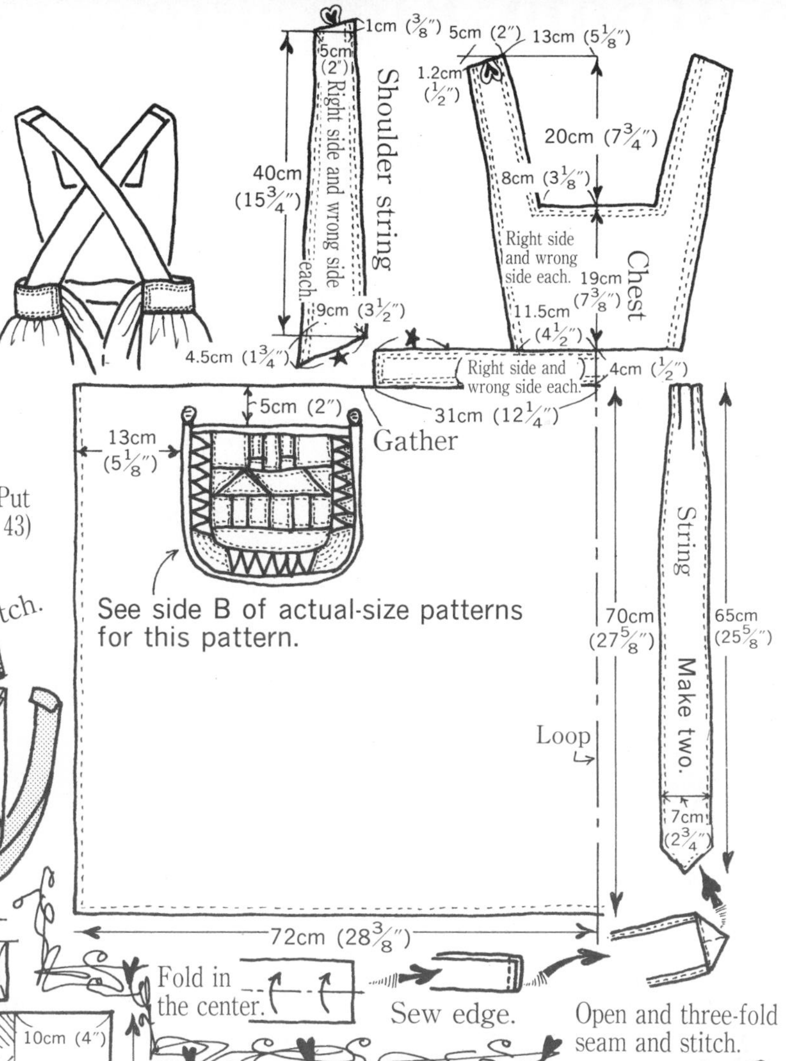

3. Make a pocket.

Sew house and put triangle on edge. Put cotton fabric and lining, baste (see p. 43) and quilt (see p. 42). Pipe upper part.

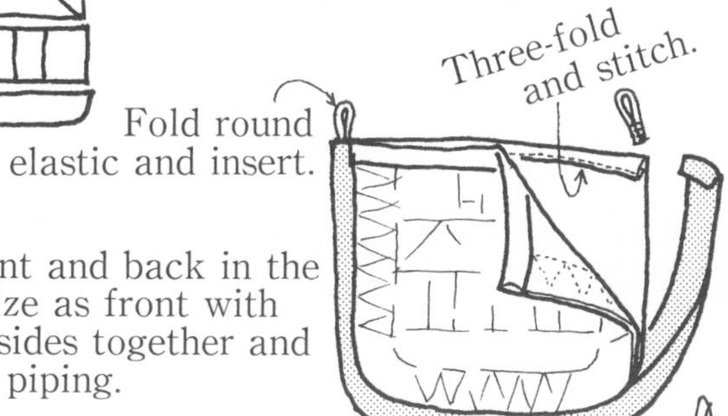

Fold round elastic and insert.

Put front and back in the same size as front with wrong sides together and sew by piping.

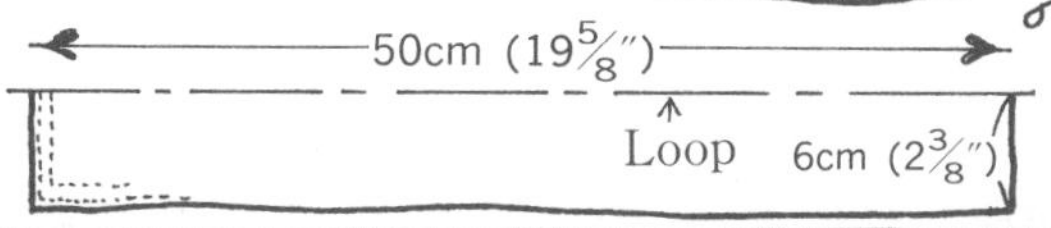

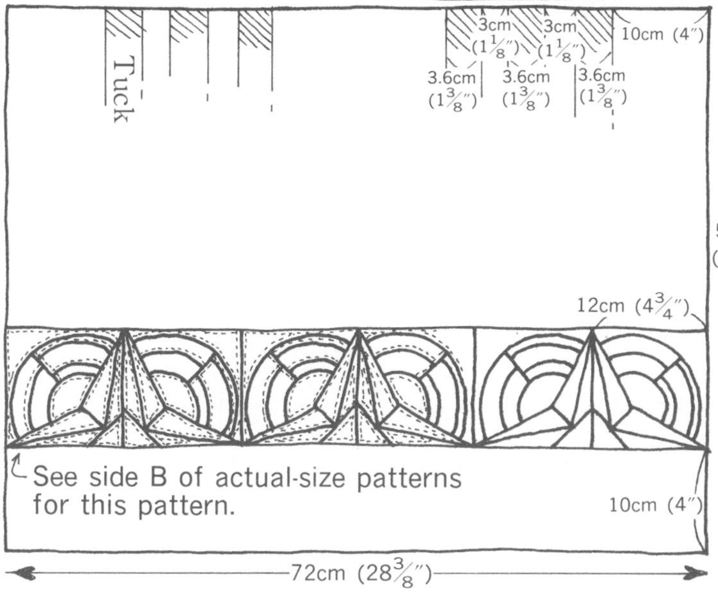

Three-fold and stitch.

1cm (⅜″) 5cm (2″) 13cm (5⅛″)
5cm (2″)
1.2cm (½″)
Right side and wrong side
Shoulder string
20cm (7¾″)
40cm (15¾″)
8cm (3⅛″)
Right side and wrong side each.
Chest
19cm (7⅜″)
9cm (3½″)
11.5cm (4½″)
4.5cm (1¾″)
Right side and wrong side each.
4cm (½″)
31cm (12¼″)
Gather

5cm (2″)
13cm (5⅛″)

See side B of actual-size patterns for this pattern.

String
Make two.
70cm (27⅝″)
65cm (25⅝″)
Loop
7cm (2¾″)

72cm (28⅜″)

Fold in the center.
Sew edge.
Open and three-fold seam and stitch.

No. 112 Apron

Sew piece worked patterns as shown and stitch finely to prevent raising.

Make tucks to make apron.

In the same way, you can put patterns on a ready-made apron.

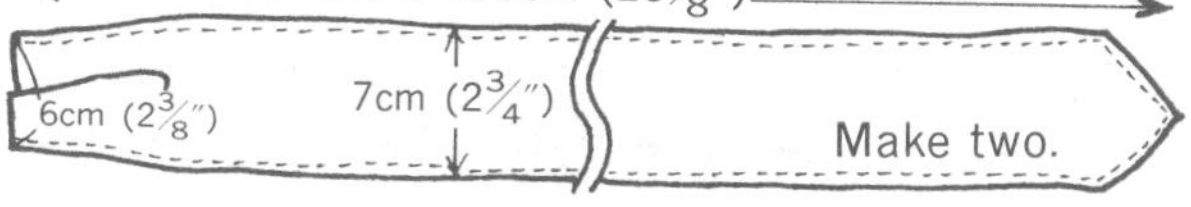

50cm (19⅝″)
Loop 6cm (2⅜″)

Tuck
3cm (1⅛″) 3cm (1⅛″) 10cm (4″)
3.6cm (1⅜″) 3.6cm (1⅜″) 3.6cm (1⅜″)

54cm (21¼″)

12cm (4¾″)

See side B of actual-size patterns for this pattern.

10cm (4″)

72cm (28⅜″)

65cm (25⅝″)
6cm (2⅜″)
7cm (2¾″)
Make two.

Cut out pieces, adding 1.5cm seam allowance, three-fold and stitch.

Make one tuck to make it 6cm wide and put onto belt.

Open the Door to Room Flooring

Duck Family can be used as door stoppers. A brick inside acts as a weight. Create a wonderful color scheme of the ducks and floor mat in varied colors.

Instructions on page 3.

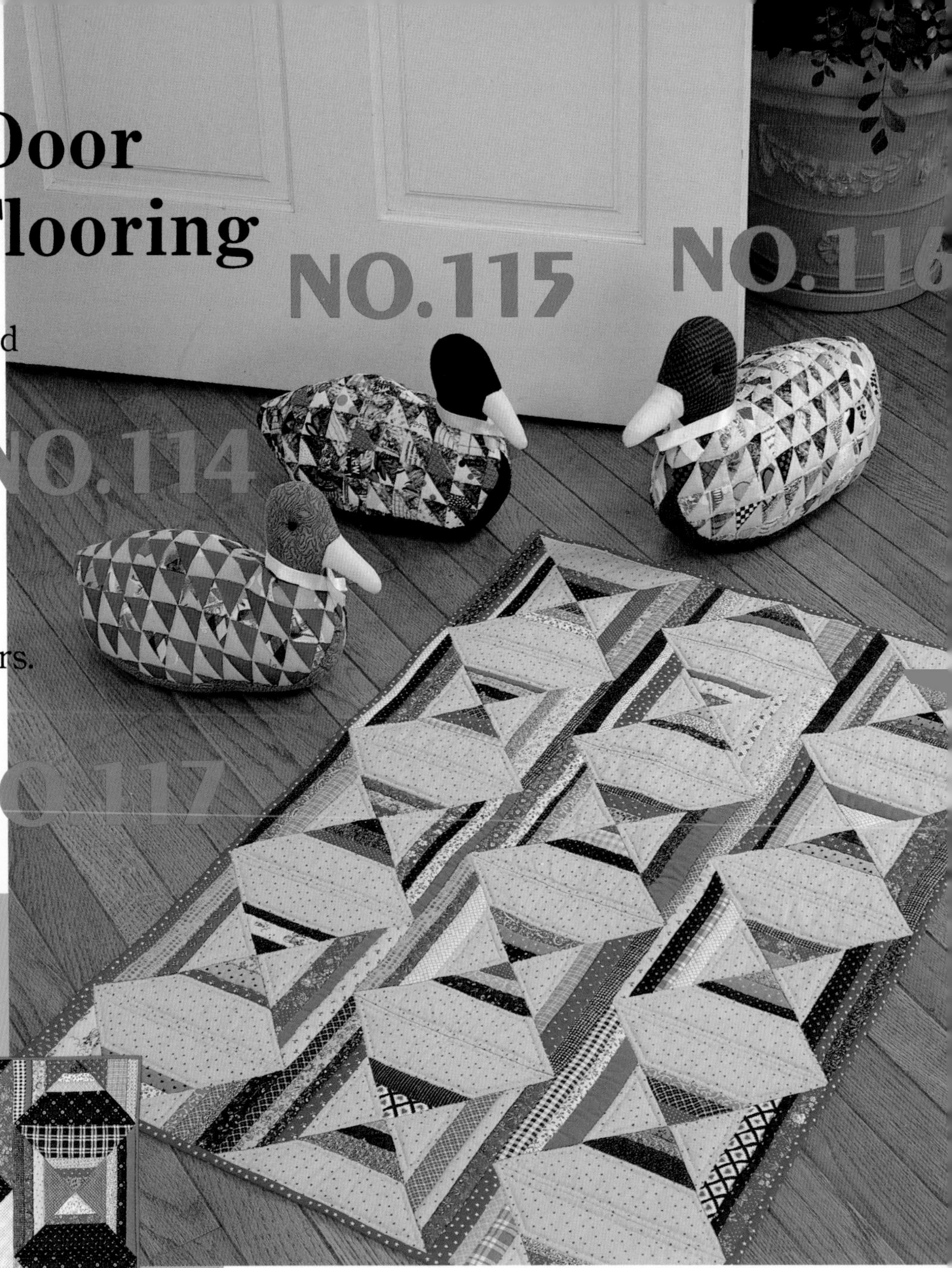

NO.115

NO.116

NO.114

NO.117

NO.118

Epilogue

Have you enjoyed the many patchworks presented here? We hope they will help create a homey atmosphere in your daily life.